The Incredible Honeymoon

Nesbit, E. (Edith), 1858-1924

Nabu Public Domain Reprints:

You are holding a reproduction of an original work published before 1923 that is in the public domain in the United States of America, and possibly other countries. You may freely copy and distribute this work as no entity (individual or corporate) has a copyright on the body of the work. This book may contain prior copyright references, and library stamps (as most of these works were scanned from library copies). These have been scanned and retained as part of the historical artifact.

This book may have occasional imperfections such as missing or blurred pages, poor pictures, errant marks, etc. that were either part of the original artifact, or were introduced by the scanning process. We believe this work is culturally important, and despite the imperfections, have elected to bring it back into print as part of our continuing commitment to the preservation of printed works worldwide. We appreciate your understanding of the imperfections in the preservation process, and hope you enjoy this valuable book.

[See page 118

They sat among the twisted tree roots, and ate and drank and were merry like children on a holiday.

THE INCREDIBLE HONEYMOON

BY

E. NESBIT

AUTHOR OF
"THE RED HOUSE" ETC.

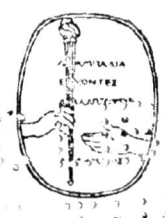

HARPER & BROTHERS PUBLISHERS
NEW YORK AND LONDON

BOOKS BY
E. NESBIT

THE INCREDIBLE HONEYMOON
   Frontispiece. Post 8vo
THE BOOK OF DRAGONS. Illustrated. 8vo
THE RED HOUSE Illustrated. Post 8vo
THE ENCHANTED CASTLE
   Illustrated Post 8vo
THE WOULDBEGOODS. Illustrated. Post 8vo

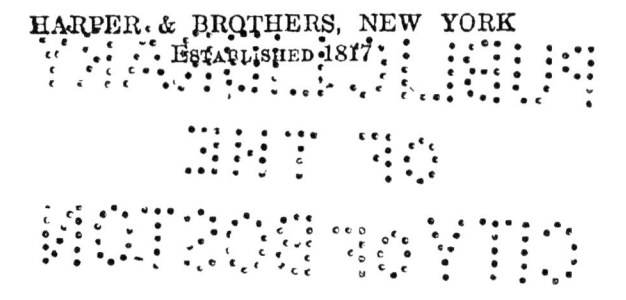

HARPER & BROTHERS, NEW YORK
Established 1817

THE INCREDIBLE HONEYMOON

Copyright, 1916, by Harper & Brothers
Printed in the United States of America
Published October, 1916

K-Q

THE INCREDIBLE HONEYMOON

I

THE BEGINNING

TO understand this story you will have to believe in the Greater Gods—Love and Youth, for example, and Adventure and Coincidence; also in the trusting heart of woman and the deceitful spirit of man. You will have to reconcile yourself to the fact that though daily you go to London by the nine-seven, returning by the five-fifteen, and have your accustomed meals at eight, one, and half-past six, there are those who take neither trains nor meals regularly. That, while nothing on earth ever happens to you, there really are on earth people to whom things do happen. Nor is the possibility of such happenings wholly a matter of the independent income—the income for which you do not work. It is a matter of the individual soul. I knew a man whose parents had placed him in that paralyzing sort of situation which is symbolized by the regular trains and the regular meals. It was quite a nice situation for some people, a situation, too, in which one was certain to "get on." But the man I knew had other dreams. He chucked his job, one fine Saturday morning in May, went for a long walk, met a tinker and bought his outfit—a wheel on wheels, a sort of barrow with a grindstone on it, and a pot for putting fire in dangling underneath. This he wheeled profitably through rural districts—so profitably that he was presently able to buy a donkey and a cart, and to sell kettles as well as mend them. He has since bought a gipsy tent; with these impediments—or helps—he travels through the pleasant country. Things are always happening to him. He has found a buried treasure; frustrated a burglary; once he rescued a lady in distress; and another time he killed a man. The background to these dramatic incidents is always the pleasant background of quiet road, blossoming hedgerows and orchards, corn-fields and meadows and lanes. He says this is the way to live. I will write down his story some day, but this is not it. I only bring him in to illustrate my point, which is that adventures do happen—to the adventurous.

THE BEGINNING

My friend the tinker has had, perhaps, more than his share of adventures, but then his is the temperament that shoots, like a willing needle, to the great magnet of melodrama. The temperamental needle of Edward Basingstoke followed the magnet of romance. In a gayer, if less comfortable, age he might have been a knight-errant, or, at least, the sympathetic squire of a knight-errant. Had he been born in the days when most people stayed at home and minded their own business he would have insisted on going out and minding other people's. Living in the days of aeroplanes, motors, telegraphy, and cinematographs, in a world noisy with the nonsense of politics and the press, he told himself that the ideal life was the life of the farmer who plowed and sowed and reaped, tended his beasts and filled his barns, and went home from his clean, quiet work to the open hearth whence the wood smoke curled up to heaven like the smoke of an altar.

Destiny, in deep perversity, was making an engineer of him. He dreamed his pastoral dreams in the deafening clangor of the shops at Crewe, but not ten thousand hammers could beat out of his brain the faith that life was really—little as one might suppose it, just looking at it from Crewe—full of the most beautiful and delicate possibilities, and that, somehow or other, people got from life what they chose to take. While he was making up his mind what he should take, he went on learning his trade. And Destiny seemed determined that he should learn nothing else. What we call Destiny is really Chance—and so far from being immutable, she is the veriest flirt and weathercock. She changed her mind about Edward—or perhaps Death, who is stronger than she, insisted and prevailed.

Just at the time when a faint dust was beginning to settle on his dreams—the sort of dust that thickens and hardens into clay and you grow cabbages in it—Death intervened to save him. It was his uncle who died, and he left a will, and by that will certain property came to Edward. When the news came he took a day to think of it, and he went to the works as usual that afternoon and the next morning. But next day at noon he laid down his tools and never took them up again. Instead he took a ticket to Oxford, appeared at the rooms of his friend, whom he surprised in slumber, and told his tale.

"And you're going to chuck the shop," said the friend, whose name was Vernon Martingale, and his father a baronet.

"I have chucked the shop," said Edward. "I chucked it at Fate as you might throw a stone at

THE BEGINNING

a dog. And that reminds me—I want a dog. Do you know of a nice dog—intelligent, good manners, self-respecting, and worthy?"

"Any particular breed?"

"Certainly not. These researches into family history are in the worst possible taste. You don't love me for my pedigree. Why should I love my dog for his?"

"I suppose you want some tea, anyhow," said Martingale.

So they had tea, and talked cricket.

"Any idea what you mean to do?" Martingale asked several times, and at last Edward answered him.

"What I mean to do," he said, "is what I always meant to do. I mean to be a farmer, and hunt, and shoot, and grow flowers. I think I shall specialize on sunflowers. They're so satisfying."

"More than you are," said Vernon. "Mean to say you're going to buy a farm and ruin yourself the moment you've got a few half-crowns to ruin yourself with?"

"I am going to be a farmer," said Basingstoke, "but first I am going to see life."

"Life? But you were always so . . ."

"I mean *that*"—Edward indicated the sunshine outside—"not getting drunk and being disreputable. I can't think why the deuce-dickens that sort of beastliness is always called seeing life. As if life were all gas, and wining, and electric light, and the things you don't talk about before ladies. No, my boy, I'm going out into the unknown—not into the night, because it happens to be afternoon—and I thought I'd just come and clasp that hand and gaze once into those eyes before I set my foot on the untrodden path of adventure. Farewell, Vernon of Martingale, good knight and true! Who knows when we shall meet again?"

"*I* don't, anyhow," said Vernon, "and that's why you're not going till the day after to-morrow, and why I insist on knowing what you mean by seeing life—and why you're going to stay till to-morrow, anyhow."

"Heaven forbid that I should criticize another man's tastes," Edward sighed, "or deprive him of any innocent enjoyment. If you want me to stay—well, I'll stay—till to-morrow. And as for what I mean by seeing life—well, I should have thought even you would have understood that. I'm going to get a stick, and a knapsack, and a dog, and a different kind of hat, and some very large boots with nails, and a new suit, only I shall wear it all night before I wear it all day. Oh, Vernon, can't you guess my simple secret?"

"He calls a walking-tour seeing life!" Vernon

THE BEGINNING

pointed out. "And who's going with you and where are you going? The Hartz Mountains?—the Carpathians?—Margate?—Trouville? What?"

"The person who is going with me," said Edward, "is the dog whom we haven't yet bought. Come along out and buy him. As to where I'm going, I shall follow the most ancient of signposts—and I know that I can't go wrong."

"You will follow—"

"My nose," Edward explained, kindly—

> "That indicator of the place to be,
> The Heaven-sent guide to beauty and to thee.

"Do you know, if you talk rot to the chaps at the works they try to understand what you mean. Like Scotchmen, you know. They think they can understand anything, no matter how shallow. Now I will say for you that you know your limitations. Let's buy the dog, my son, and get a canoe."

They did. And the dog upset the canoe.

II

MAKING AN AEROPLANE

THE Five Bells was asleep; asleep, at least, was the face with which it met the world. In the brick-floored kitchen, out of sight and hearing of the road, the maid was singing as she sluiced the bricks with a white mop; but if she and her mop had been state secrets, matters of life and death, they could not have been more safely hidden from any chance passer. In the bar the landlord was asleep behind the *Lewes Gazette and South Coast Journal.* In the parlor the landlady was asleep behind a screen of geraniums and campanulas. The ornamental clock on the mantelpiece said, most untruly, ten minutes to eight. Really it was four o'clock, the sleepiest hour in the day. The flies buzzed in the parlor window; in the bar the wasps buzzed in the bottle that had seemed so sweet a bourn to each as it drifted in from the out-of-door heat to the cool darkness of the sanded bar.

MAKING AN AEROPLANE

On the broad, white door-step the old cat slept, his person nicely adjusted to the sun and shade, his flanks in the sunshine and his head in the shadow of the porch. The white blind of the window swelled out, now and then, like a sail, because in this sort of weather one leaves all doors and windows open. In the yard some one had drawn a bucket of water—the brown oak and the brown iron of the bucket were still wet, and still wet the trail it had made where it was carried to the old bath that the chickens drank from. But the trail was drying quickly, and the hens, having had their drink, had gone to sleep in the hollows they had scooped for themselves in the dust of their inclosure. Some one had been chopping wood, for a few chips lay round the block, in which the bill was stuck by its sharp edge. The man who attended to the wood and water was asleep, standing against the ladder that led from the stable to the hay-loft—a convenient position, and, if you were wanted in a hurry, not compromising, as lying down would be.

To right and left the road stretched, very white and shining, between dusty hedgerows and scattered cottages whose drawn blinds looked like the eyelids of sleepers. The whole village was asleep, it seemed—only a boy and a dog were awake. The boy had not gone to school because he had torn his every-day trousers on a nail in the stable. To wear his Sunday trousers was, of course, out of the question. And to mend the every-day trousers would take time. So Tommy was put to bed, nominally as a punishment for not looking where he was going—a most unfair implication, for the nail had attacked him in the rear. Children do not go to sleep when they are put to bed as a punishment. They cry, if their spirit has been broken by unkindness; if not, they lie and meditate mischief. Tommy waited till the afternoon silence settled on the house, and then very carefully and slowly crept down the stairs in his nightshirt, dodged Gladys and the mop, and reached the larder. Here he secured a flead-cake, a raisin-cake, and an apple, dodged Gladys again, and reached the back door, where he stood looking out at the yard. It would be silly to go back to bed. Mother would not be awake for a good half-hour yet. There would be time to get to the stable, climb into the loft, and eat his booty there. It would be safer, in one way, and in another more adventurous.

He stooped till his head was below the kitchen window and crept by, skirting the walls of the yard till he reached the stable door, and next moment was safe in the half-darkness where the sunlight through the cracks of the door made dusty

MAKING AN AEROPLANE

shafts of radiance. The familiar smell of hay and horses charmed him, as it always did. Ah, there was Robert, asleep as usual. Well, even if Robert woke, he could be trusted not to tell. Tommy climbed into the manger of one of the empty stalls, and just as he got his knee on it some one behind pushed him with sudden and incredible violence. He fell heavily, dropped his plunder, and found himself involved in the enthusiastic embraces of a large, strange, white dog, which in one breathless instant licked his face all over, trampled on his stomach, made two mouthfuls of the flead-cake and the raisin-cake, rolled the apple in the muck of the stable, snorted in a sort of brutal ecstasy, and bolted heavily out into the sunshine.

It was too much. The sudden and brutal attack overcame all considerations of prudence. Tommy forgot where he was, and why; the dangers of his situation were nothing beside the outrage of this unprovoked assault and theft. Robert was awakening slowly. If he had been awake before he might have repulsed the enemy. Tommy opened his mouth to howl, but the howl changed to a scream, for there was the dog back again, snuffing loudly in the straw and fawning at Tommy as on an old and valued friend.

"Charles!" a stern voice called from the yard, "come here, sir."

THE INCREDIBLE HONEYMOON

The dog wagged a muscular tail and grinned at Tommy, as though inviting him to share the joke. The stable door was darkened by a form. Even in the difficulties of repulsing the dog's attention without irritating it, the child found time to be glad that the darkening form was that of a stranger.

"Call him off, if he's your dog," Tommy urged, thickly, backing against the manger.

"Might as well call him off, sir," Robert—now almost awake—conceded.

The stranger stepped forward, a snap clicked, and Charles, still widely smiling, was straining at the end of a leathern thong.

"I hope he didn't frighten you," said the stranger.

"He bunted at me with his great head," said Tommy, with half a sob, "and then he eat up what I'd got, and hooked it off again afore you could say knife."

"What had you got?"

"Nothing," said Tommy, remembering caution, "at least—"

"The jingling of the guinea heals," said the stranger, incomprehensibly. "Would sixpence be any comfort to you?"

Tommy's eyes answered, and the stranger held it out.

MAKING AN AEROPLANE

"Thank you, sir," said Tommy, and added, in close imitation of his father's manner to thirsty travelers, "Going far to-day, sir?"

"I was thinking," said the stranger, "of putting up here."

"Then," said Tommy, with great presence of mind, "please don't say anything to them about the dog eating—what he did eat—nor me being here in my shirt, nor about Robert being asleep. If you'll go round to the front, sir, you'll find the bar, and that 'll give me a chance to slip back to bed, sir, if you'd be so kind."

"I see," said the stranger, "you were sent to bed."

"In punishment like," said Tommy, "so you see I don't want to . . ."

"Exactly. An unobserved retreat. I will draw the enemy's fire from the front premises. Come, Charles."

Charles obeyed, only pausing to entangle the lead in the handle of a shovel and to bring this down upon the feet of Robert, to upset a sieve of chaff and run between his master's legs with a sudden violence which, but for the support of the door-post, would have thrown him to the ground.

"Nice-spoken young man," said Robert. "Now, young Tommy, you cut along back where you belong. I'll be asking Gladys the time to keep her off of the back door while you slips in, you young limb."

He strolled across to the window as Tommy's bare feet trod the sun-warmed bricks to the back door. As the child crept up the stairs he heard the stranger's voice in the bar.

"Sixpence," said Tommy, in ecstasy, "and him going to put up here." He cuddled down into his bed well satisfied with the afternoon's adventure. Adventures are, indeed, to the adventurous.

"If I'd 'a' bin a good boy and stayed in bed nothing wouldn't have happened," was how he put it to himself.

Meanwhile the stranger, encumbered by the striving Charles, was "being shown the rooms"— the bare, much-scrubbed bedroom, the all-too-full and too-carpeted parlor.

"They are exactly what I want," he said, and so won the heart of his hostess.

When Tommy, his trousers restored, came down to tea he was warned not to go clamping about in his boots, because there was a gentleman in the parlor. Tommy fingered the sixpence in his pocket and said nothing; his mouth was, indeed, far too full for words.

That evening in the parched orchard behind the house Tommy came edging shyly toward the

MAKING AN AEROPLANE

stranger as he lounged under the trees smoking a fat pipe.

"Hullo, young man!" was the greeting. "Come here and talk to me."

Tommy dumbly drew near.

"Got your trousers back, I see," said the stranger, genially.

Tommy admitted it with a grunt. The stranger nodded and took his pipe out of his mouth.

"Ever see a pig?" he asked.

Tommy grunted again.

"I see you have. You speak their language awfully well." The stranger uttered a sound which Tommy recognized and smiled to hear. "That's what the pigs say," said the stranger. "Agreeable little boys who have recovered their trousers say 'Yes' or 'No' when their friends ask them questions. Don't they?"

"I dun'no'," said Tommy.

"Oh yes, you do. Because I've told you. Now what would you like to do?"

"I dun'no'."

"I can't tell you that you know, because I don't know myself. But I'll put it to you like this: If you can make up your mind to talk the language of agreeable little boys who have recovered their trousers, I am disposed to endure your company and even to assist you in any play you may have in hand. But I can't associate with a person who grunts at me. If you want to grunt, go and grunt at some one who likes it. I don't."

"I didn't go for to," Tommy urged.

"Handsomely admitted. I accept your apology. You don't know what you'd like to do, I say. Well, is there anything you'd like to *have?* I'm living the idle life, Tommy, and my hands are beginning to ache for want of something to do. I want to make something. Ever make anything?"

"I made a rabbit-hutch, onst," Tommy owned, "but the door warn't straight on her hinges. And I tried a kite—but it stuck to me and come to bits afore ever it was dry."

"Look here," said the stranger, sitting up, "what about a kite? I could make you a kite as big as a house or a fire-balloon. Would you like that?"

Tommy began a grunt, pretended that it had been a cough, and turned that into, "Yes, please, sir."

"We must restrain Charles," said the stranger, turning to the large white dog, who sat with feet firmly planted, smiling a wide, pink smile, "or this kite will certainly stick to *him* and come to pieces afore *it's* dry. Where's the shop?"

"Down street," said Tommy. "I could pop down street in a minute for the paper and things."

MAKING AN AEROPLANE

"Sure you'd rather have a kite than anything else?"

Tommy hesitated, and then said of course he'd rather have a hairyplane, but he supposed the stranger couldn't.

To which the stranger startlingly replied, "Oh, couldn't I, my boy! Father got a horse and trap?" he went on. And from that moment the most wonderful four days of Tommy's life moved forward majestically without pause or let.

To drive into Eastbourne with the gentleman—rather slow the old horse was, but it was the best trap—to hold the reins outside important and unusual shops, including the Eastbourne Motor-Car Company and the telegraph-office at the station; to be taken to dinner at a fine hotel with flowers in all the windows, and real waiters dressed exactly like the gentlemen who sang at the school concert, white ties and all—or just like the butler at Mr. Ferney's who had the training-stables—and such things to eat as Tommy "never did."

The horse and trap were put up at Mr. Pettigrew's Livery and Bait Stables, in itself an act of unheard-of daring and extravagance. And after dinner the stranger got a motor-car—a real private one—none of your red flags and mustn't ride on the front seat, where, in fact, he and the

THE INCREDIBLE HONEYMOON

stranger did, with great dash and daring, actually ride. And they went to Pevensy and Hurstmonceau and Hastings, and the stranger told Tommy stories about the places, so that history was never quite itself again to Tommy. Then back to Eastbourne, to call again at the unusual shops, as well as at one of the more usual character, where the stranger bought toffee and buns and cake and peppermint creams; to get a parcel from the station, and so home round the feet of the downs in the pleasant-colored evening, with the dust white on the hedges, and the furze in flower, and the skylarks singing "fit to bu'st theirselves," as Tommy pointed out when the stranger called his attention to the little, dark, singing specks against the clear sky, the old white horse going at a spanking pace. No one would have believed he had it in him, compared to what he was in the morning; and drawing up very short and sharp in front of the porch—no driving into the yard and just calling for Robert—and father himself coming out to take the reins. Oh, that was a day!

To the stranger, also, whose name, it will surprise you little to learn, was Edward Basingstoke, the home-coming was not without charm. The day before he had been welcomed as a guest; now he was welcomed as a friend, one who had taken Tommy for an outing and spent money on him

MAKING AN AEROPLANE

like water. Any one could see that from the parcels the child had his arms full of.

Robert in the stable, hearing the return, and heartened by the unmistakable attitude of the family, loosened Charles from the taut chain at whose end he had choked all day, and sent him flying like a large white bullet into the bar, where his master was standing. Charles knocked over a table and three glasses, trod on the edge of a spittoon and upset it, and the landlord said it didn't matter! Could any reception have been more warmly welcoming?

It charmed Edward so much that he said, "When Tommy's face is washed, might he have tea with me to finish up the day?"

And this, too, happened. And after tea, when Charles had been partially calmed by five whole buns, eaten in five eager mouthfuls, they undid the parcels, and Tommy reveled in the tools and metals, the wood, the canvas, the dozen other things he knew neither the names nor the uses of. And when it was time to say good night and they had said it, Tommy wanted to say something else. He stood by the parlor door, shuffling his boots and looking with blue, adoring eyes at the stranger.

"I say," he said.

"Well, what *do* you say?"

"I say," was still all that Tommy said.

"Yes, I hear you do. But what?"

"I'm right-down glad you come here to stay, instead of going on to Wilmington, like what you might have," was the most Tommy could do. Then he added, after a fierce, brief struggle between affection and shyness: "I do take it very kind, sir—and the peppermints, and all. Good night, sir."

It was the happiest day Edward had spent since he left Crewe.

And next day they began to make the aeroplane. I do not know how toy aeroplanes are made. There may be a hundred ways of making them. If there are, Mr. Basingstoke knew at least one of these ways, and it was quite a good way, too. The village carpenter and the village blacksmith each was visited—I know that—and a good deal of the work was done at the carpenter's bench. And at the end of the third day the toy was ready.

"We'll fly it in the morning," said Mr. Basingstoke. "Are you glad it's done? Sure you wouldn't have liked a kite better?"

"Not by long chalks," was Tommy's fervent answer.

The little aeroplane sat on the little stand the carpenter had made for it, shiny with varnish, white with canvas, glittering in all its metal mysteries.

MAKING AN AEROPLANE

"Jiminy!" said Tommy, awe-stricken at his own good fortune, "I didn't know anybody could be so clever as what you are."

Edward Basingstoke, as he went to bed, wondered whether, after all, he could spend his money to any better purpose than going about the country making aeroplanes to please little boys.

III

EDEN

WHEN you have made an aeroplane, the next thing is to make it fly. And however agreeable an admiring audience may be while one is fiddling with definite and concrete objects of wood, canvas, and metal, one is apt, for the flight itself—the great flight, the flight by which the aeroplane shall stand or fall—to desire solitude.

That was why Edward drew the yellow blind up and the dimity curtain aside and turned his bed round, so that the sun at its first rising should strike through his dreams and awaken him. The sun did exactly what it was expected to do, and Edward awoke saying "Bother" before he remembered that "Bother" was not at all what he meant. Then he got up and splashed gently, so as not to break the audible sleep of the people in the next room, stole down the creaking, twisted stairs in his tennis-shoes, soft-footed as a cat, drew the bolts of the back door, and slipped out, closing the door noiselessly behind him. He was careful to draw the bolt into its place again by means of a bit of fishing-line. You can do this quite easily with an old door that does not fit very closely—if you are careful to mark with chalk on the outside of the door, as Edward did, the exact place where the bolt is. Having thus secured the door against passing tramps or burglars, he went out across the highroad, soft with thick, white dust, where the dew lay on hedge and grassy border, and the sun made diamonds of the dew. Charles, choking himself in the stable, grew faint with distance.

Beyond the village was a meadow suited to his needs. It was bordered on one side by a high red-brick wall, above whose moss-grown coping the rounded shapes of trees leaned. A wood edged it on two other sides, and in the front was a road.

Here he made his preparations, wound up his machine, and, after one or two false starts, got it going. He meant to fly it like a kite, and to this end he had tied one end of a ball of fine twine to the middle of its body. Now he raised it above his head and launched it. The little creature rose like a bird; the ball of string leaped and jumped between his feet, as he paid out the line; the whirring wings hung poised a second, at the level of the tree-tops, and then, caught by the wind, sailed straight toward the red wall, burrowed into the trees, and stopped. He ran toward the wall, winding up the string, and stood below, looking up. He could not see the winged loose thing. He tweaked the string and his tweak was met with uncompromising resistance. The aeroplane had stuck in a chestnut-tree, and hung there, buzzing.

Edward measured the wall with his eye. It was an old wall, of soft red brick, from which the mortar had fallen away. In its crannies moss grew, and ragged-robin and ground-ivy hung their delicate veil in the angles of its buttresses—little ferns and wall-flowers run to seed marked its courses, the yellow snapdragon which English children call toad-flax flaunted its pure sulphur-colored plumes from the ledge below the coping. An architect would have said that the wall wanted pointing; a builder would have pointed it—an artist would have painted it. To an engineer in grief for a lost toy the wall presented itself as an obstacle to be climbed. He climbed it.

He thrust the string into his jacket pocket, and presently set hand and foot to the hold that the worn wall afforded. In half a minute he was astride the coping; next moment he had swung by his hands and let himself go on the wall's other side. It was a longer drop than he expected; it jarred him a little, and his hat tumbled off. As he picked this up he noticed that the wall on the inside had been newly pointed. The trees were a good thirty feet from the wall. There would be no getting back by the way he had come. He must find a gate. Meantime the little aeroplane's buzzing had grown faint and ceased. But the twine led him to the tree, as the silken clue led Queen Eleanor to the tower of Fair Rosamond. The next thing was to climb the tree and bring down the truant toy.

The park spread smooth and green before him—the green smoothness that comes only to English grass growing where grass has been these many years. Quiet trees dotted the smooth greenness—thickening about the house, whose many chimneys, red and twisted, rose smokeless above the clustered green. Nothing moved in all the park, where the sun drank the dew; birds stirred and twittered in the branches—that was all. The little aeroplane had stopped its buzzing. Edward was moved to thank Fate that he had not brought Charles. Also he was glad that this trespass of his had happened so early. He would get down the aeroplane and quietly go out by the lodge gate. Even if locked, it would be climbable.

The chestnut-tree, however, had to be climbed

first. It was easy enough, though the leaves baffled him a little, so that it was some time before he saw the desired gleam of metal and canvas among the dappled foliage. Also, it was not quite easy to get the thing down without injuring it, and one had to go slowly.

He lowered it, at last, by its string to the ground from the lowest branch, then moved along a little, hung by his hands, and dropped.

He picked up the toy and turned to go. "Oh!" he said, without meaning to. And, "I beg your pardon," without quite knowing what for.

Because, as he turned he came face to face with a vision, the last one would have expected to see in an English park at early day. A girl in a Burmese coat, red as poppies, with gold-embroidered hem a foot deep. Her dress was white. Her eyes were dark, her face palely bright, and behind her dark head a golden-green Japanese umbrella made a great ridged halo.

"I beg your pardon," said Edward again, and understood that it was because he was, after all, trespassing.

"I should think you did," said the vision, crossly. "What on earth do you mean by it? How did you get in?"

Edward, standing a little awkwardly with the aeroplane in his hands, looked toward the wall.

EDEN

"I came over after this," he said. "I'm very sorry. I was flying the thing and it stuck in the tree. If you'll tell me the way to the lodge, I'll—I hope I didn't scare you."

"I couldn't think what it was," she answered, a little less crossly. "I saw the tree tossing about as if—as if it had gone mad."

"And you thought of dryads and hastened to the spot. And it was only an idiot and his aeroplane. I say—I *am* sorry—"

"You can't help not being a dryad," she said, and now she smiled, and her smile transformed her face as sunlight does a landscape. "What I really thought you were was a tramp. Only tramps never climb trees. I couldn't think how you got in here, though. Tramps never climb walls. They get in sometimes through the oak fence beyond the plantations."

"It was very intrepid of you to face a tramp," he said.

"Oh, I love tramps," she said; "they're always quite nice to you if you don't bully them or patronize them. There were two jolly ones last week, and I talked to them, and they made tea out in the road, you know, and gave me a cup over the fence. It *was* nasty." She shuddered a little. "But I liked it awfully, all the same," she added. "I wish I were a tramp."

THE INCREDIBLE HONEYMOON

"It's not a bad life," said he.

"It's *the* life," she said, enthusiastically. "No ties, no responsibilities—no nasty furniture and hateful ornaments—you just go where you like and do what you like; and when you don't like where you are, you go somewhere else; and when you don't like what you're doing, you needn't go on doing it."

"Those are very irresponsible sentiments—for a lady."

"I know. That's why I think it's so dull being a woman. Men can do whatever they want to."

"Only if they haven't their living to earn," said Edward, not quite so much to himself as he would have liked.

There was a little pause, and then, still less himself, he blundered into, "I say, it is jolly of you to talk to me like this."

She froze at once. "I forgot," she said, "that we had not been introduced. Thank you for reminding me."

Edward's better self was now wholly lost, and what was left of him could find nothing better to answer than, "Oh, I say!"

"What I ought to have said," she went on, her face a mask of cold politeness, "is that you can't possibly get out by the lodge. There are fierce dogs. And the lodge-keepers are worse than the dogs. If you will follow me—at a distance, for fear I should begin to talk to you again—I'll show you where the gardener's ladder is, and you can put it up against the wall and get out that way."

"Couldn't I get out where the tramps get in?" he asked, humbly. "I don't like to trouble you."

"Not from here. We should have to pass close by the house."

The "we" gave him courage. "I say—do forgive me," he said.

"There's nothing to forgive," said she.

"Oh, but do," he said, "if you'd only see it! It was just because it was so wonderful and splendid to have met you like this . . . and to have you talk to me as you do to the other tramps."

"You're not a tramp," she said, "and I ought not to have forgotten it."

"But I am," said he, "it's just what I really and truly am."

"Come and get the ladder," said she, and moved toward the wall.

"Not unless you forgive me. I won't," he added, plucking up a little spirit, "be indebted for ladders to people who won't forgive a man because he speaks the truth clumsily."

"Come," she said, looking back over her shoulder.

THE INCREDIBLE HONEYMOON

"No," he said, obstinately, not moving. "Not unless you forgive me."

"It can't possibly matter to you whether I forgive you or not," she turned to say it. And as she spoke there came to Edward quite suddenly and quite unmistakably the knowledge that it did matter. Sometimes glimpses do thus suddenly and strangely come to us—and that by some magic inner light that is not reason we know things that by the light of reason we could never know.

"Look here," he said. "I'll go after that ladder in a minute. But first I've got something to say to you. Don't be angry, because I've got to say it. Do you know that just now—just before I said that stupid thing that offended you—you were talking to me as though you'd known me all your life?"

"You needn't rub it in," she said.

"Do you know why that is? It's because you *are* going to know me all your life. I'm perfectly certain of it. Somehow or other, it's true. We're going to be friends. I sha'n't need to say again how jolly it is of you to talk to me. We shall take all that as a matter of course. People aren't pitchforked into meetings like this for nothing. I'm glad I said that. I'm glad you were angry with me for saying it. If you hadn't I might just have gone away and not known till I got outside

EDEN

—and then it would have been a deuce and all of a business to get hold of you again. But now I know. And you know, too. When shall I see you again? Never mind about forgiving me. Just tell me when I shall see you again. And then I'll go."

"You must be mad," was all she could find to say. She had furled her sunshade and was smoothing its bamboo ribs with pink fingers.

"You'll be able to find out whether I'm mad, you know, when you see me again. As a matter of fact—which seems maddest, when you meet some one you want to talk to, to go away without talking or to insist on talk and more talk? And you can't say you didn't want to talk to me, because you know you did. Look here, meet me to-morrow morning again—will you?"

"Certainly not."

"You'll be sorry if you don't. We're like two travelers who have collected all sorts of wonderful things in foreign countries. We long to show each other our collections—all the things we've thought and dreamed. If we'd been what you call introduced, perhaps we shouldn't have found this out. But as it is, we know it."

"Speak for yourself," she said.

"Thank you," he said, seriously. "I will. Will you sit down for ten minutes? This tree-root was

THE INCREDIBLE HONEYMOON

made for you to sit down on for ten minutes, and I will speak for myself."

"I can't," she said, and her voice—there was hurry in it, and indecision, but the ice had gone. "You must come at once for that ladder. It's getting more dangerous every moment. If any one saw you here there'd be an awful row."

"For you?"

"Yes, for me. Come on."

He followed her along the wall under the chestnuts. There was no more spoken words till they came to the ladder.

Then, "Right," he said. "Thank you. Good-by." And set the ladder against the wall.

"Good-by," said she. "I'll hand the aeroplane up to you?"

"Stand clear," he said, half-way up the ladder. "I'll give it a sideways tip from the top—it'll fall into its place. It's too heavy for you to lift. Good-by."

He had reached the top of the wall. She stood below, looking up at him.

"There won't be any row now?"

"No. It's quite safe."

"Then have you nothing to say?"

"Nothing. Yes, I have. I will come to-morrow. You'll misunderstand everything if I don't."

"Thank you," he said.

EDEN

She came up the ladder, two steps, then handed him his toy. Then the ladder fell with a soft thud among the moss and earth and dead leaves; his head showed a moment above the wall, then vanished.

He went thoughtfully through the dewy grass, along the road, and back to his inn.

Tommy met him by the horse-trough. "You been flying it?" he asked, breathlessly.

"Yes. She went like a bird."

"How far did she go?" Tommy asked.

"I don't quite know," said Edward, quite truly, "how far she went. I shall know better to-morrow."

IV

THE SOUTH DOWNS

THE day was long. Though the aeroplane flew to admiration, though Tommy adored him and all his works, though the skylarks sang, and the downs were drenched in sunshine, Edward Basingstoke admitted to himself, before half its length was known to him, that the day was long.

He climbed the cliff above Cuckmere and sat in the sunshine there, where the gulls flashed white wings and screamed like babies; he watched the tide, milk-white with the fallen chalk of England's edge, come sousing in over the brown, seaweed-covered rocks; he felt the crisp warmth of the dry turf under his hand, and smelt the sweet smell of the thyme and the furze and the sea, and it was all good. But it was long. And, for the first time in his life, being alone was lonely.

And for the second time since the day when Charles, bounding at him from among the clean straw of an Oxford stable, had bounded into his affections, he had left that strenuous dog behind.

THE SOUTH DOWNS

He got out his road map and spread it in the sun—with stones at the corners to cheat the wind that, on those Downs, never sleeps—and tried to believe that he was planning his itinerary, and even to pretend to himself that he should start to-morrow and walk to Lewes. But instead his eyes followed the map's indication of the road to that meadow where the red wall was, and presently he found that he was no longer looking at the map, but at the book of memory, and most at the pictures painted there only that morning. Already it seemed a very long time ago.

"I am afraid," said Mr. Basingstoke, alone at the cliff's edge, "that this time it really is *it*. It's different from what I thought. It's confoundedly unsettling."

Like all healthy young men, he had always desired and intended to fall in love; he had even courted the experience, and honestly tried to lose his heart, but with a singular lack of success. In the girls he had met he had found gaiety, good looks, and a certain vague and general attractiveness—the common attribute of youth and girlhood—but nothing that even began to transfigure the world as his poets taught him that love should transfigure it. The little, trivial emotions which he had found in pressing hands and gazing into eyes had never lured him further than the gaze and the hand-clasp. Yet he had thought himself to be in love more than once.

"Or perhaps this isn't the real thing, either," he tried to reassure himself. "How could it be?"

Then he explained to himself, as he had often explained to Vernon, that love at first sight was impossible. Love, he had held and proclaimed, was not the result of the mere attraction exercised by beauty—it was the response of mind to mind, the admiration of character and qualities—the satisfaction of one's nature by the mental and moral attributes of the beloved. That was not exactly how he had put it, but that was what he had meant. And now—he had seen a girl once, for ten minutes, and already he could think of nothing else. Even if he thought of something else he could perceive the thought of her behind those other thoughts, waiting, alluring, and sure of itself, to fill his mind the moment he let it in.

"Idiot," he said at last, got up from the turf, and pocketed the map, "to-morrow she'll be quite ordinary and just like any other girl. You go for a long walk, young-fellow-my-lad, and think out a water-mill for Tommy."

This had, indeed, been more than half promised. Mr. Basingstoke was one of those persons whom their friends call thorough; their enemies say that they carry everything too far. If he did a thing at all, he liked to do it thoroughly. If he wrote a duty-letter to an aunt, he wrote a long one, and made it amusing. As often as not he would illustrate it with little pictures. If he gave a shilling to a beggar he would immediately add tobacco and agreeable conversation. One of his first acts, on coming into his inheritance, had been to pension his old nurse, who was poor and a widow with far too many children—too many, because she was a widow and poor and had to go out to work instead of looking after her family, as she wanted to do. Any one else would have written and told her she was to have two pounds a week as long as she lived. Edward sent her a large box of hot-house flowers—her birthday happening to occur at about that date—the most expensive and beautiful flowers he could find, anonymously. Then he sent her a fat hamper bursting with excellent things to eat and drink—and a box of toys and clothes for the children. The lady who "served" him with the clothes was amused at his choice—but approved it. And in the end he told his solicitors—smiling to himself at the novel possession—to write and tell the woman that an old employer had secured her an annuity. Later he went down to see her, to find her incredibly happy and prosperous, and to hear the wonderful and mysterious tale. So now, in the case of Tommy, most people would have thought an aeroplane and a motor-ride as much as any little boy could expect. But Mr. Basingstoke liked to give people much more than they could expect. It was not enough to give them enough. He liked to give a feast.

That evening after tea, Tommy breathing hard on the back of his neck, he sketched the water-wheel with the highest degree of precision and a superfluous wealth of detail. But the thought was with him through it all.

Next morning he went to the trysting-place, through the fresh, sweet morning. He climbed the wall, sat down on the log, and waited. He waited an hour, and she did not come. It says a good deal for his tenacity of purpose that when he went home he began at once on the water-wheel.

In the afternoon he took Charles out for a walk. Charles chased and killed a hen, and was butted by a goat, before they reached the end of the street; knocked a leg of mutton off the block at the butcher's in the next village; bit the rural police to the very undershirt, and also to the tune of ten compensating shillings; and was run over by a bicycle, which twisted its pedal in the consequent fall, and grazed its rider's hands and trousers knees. After each adventure Charles was firmly punished, but, though chastised, he was not chastened, and when they met a dog-cart coming slowly down a hill he was quite ready to run in front of it, barking and leaping at the horse's nose. The horse, which appeared to Charles's master to be a thoroughbred, shied. There was a whirl of dust and hoofs and brown flank, a cry from the driver—another cry, a fierce bark from Charles, ending in a howl of agony—the next instant the horse had bolted and Edward was left in the dusty road, Charles writhing in the dust, and the dog-cart almost out of sight.

"Charles, old man—Charles, lie still, can't you? Let me see if you're hurt."

He stooped, and as he stooped Charles did lie still.

His master lifted the heavy, muscular body that had been so full of life and energy. It lay limp and lifeless, head and hind-quarters drooping over his arm like a wet shawl.

Basingstoke sat down on the roadside with the dog across his knees. For him the light of life was out. Men do not cry, of course, as women do when their dogs die, but he could not see very clearly. Presently he found himself face to face with that question, always so disconcerting, even to criminals—what to do with the body. He was miles from his inn, and Charles was no light weight. He could not leave the dog in the road. His friend must have decent burial. There was nothing for it but to wait till some cart should come by and then to ask for a lift.

So he sat there, thinking such thoughts as men do think in adversity. After a calamity, when the first excitement of horror dies down, one always says, "How different everything was yesterday!" and Mr. Basingstoke said what we all say. Yesterday Charles was alive and well, and his master had not taken him out because he wanted to be at leisure to think—he realized that now—about the girl whom he was to have met to-day. And he had not met the girl. And Charles was dead.

"I wish I hadn't left you at home yesterday, old boy," said Mr. Basingstoke.

And then came the sound of hoofs, and he prepared to stop the vehicle, whatever it was, and beg for a lift for himself and what he carried. But when the wheels came near and he saw that it was the very cart that had run over Charles he sat down again and kept his eyes on the ground. It wasn't their fault, of course, but still. . . .

The cart stopped and some one was saying: "I hope the dog isn't much hurt." A hard, cold voice it was.

Edward got out his hand from under Charles to take his hat off, and said: "My dog is dead."

THE SOUTH DOWNS

"I am extremely sorry, but it was the dog's fault," said the voice, aggressively.

"Yes," said Edward.

"There's nothing to be done," said the voice. "It was nearly a nasty accident for us."

"I apologize for my dog's conduct," said Edward, formally.

And then came another voice, "But, Aunt Loo, can't we *do* anything?"

Of course you will have known all along whose voice that would be. Edward was less discerning. He had been far too much occupied with Charles and the horse to do more than realize that the two people in the cart were women—and now when he heard again the voice that had talked to him yesterday in the freshness of the morning, the shock sent his blood surging. He looked up—face, neck, ears were burning. Men do not blush, but if they did you would have said that Mr. Basingstoke blushed in that hour.

He looked up. Holding the reins was a hard, angular woman of fifty, the sort that plays golf and billiards and is perfectly competent with horses. Beside her sat the girl, and under her white hat the crimson of her face matched his own. The distress he felt at this unpropitious coincidence deepened his color. Hers deepened, too.

"You can't do anything, thank you," he said, just a moment too late. For his pause had given the aunt time to look from one to the other.

"Oh!" she said, shortly.

The girl spoke, also just too late.

"At least, let us take the poor, dear dog home for you," she said.

"By all means," said the aunt, with an air of finality. "Where shall we leave it?"

"I am at the Five Bells, in Jevington," said Edward, and was thankful to feel his ears a shade less fiery.

"I see," said the aunt, with hideous significance. "Put it in at the back, will you?"

She spoke as though Charles were a purchase she had just made and Mr. Basingstoke the shopman.

He would have liked to refuse, but how dear of Her to suggest it. "Thank you," he said, and came through the dust to the back of the cart.

Almost before he had replaced the second pin the cart moved, and he was left alone in the white road.

The way home was long and dismal—its only incident the finding of a little white handkerchief in the dust about a mile from the scene of the tragedy. It was softly scented. Of course it might be Aunt Loo's handkerchief, but he pre-

THE SOUTH DOWNS

ferred to think that it was Hers. He shook the dust from it and put it in his pocket. As he came down the village street he remembered how, only yesterday, he had heard, just here by the saddler's, that strangled, choking bark which betokened Charles's recognition of his master's approach. Well, there would be no such barking welcome for him now.

Some other dog was choking and barking, though, and in that very stable where Charles had choked and barked. And Charles's body would have been put in the stable, no doubt. He would go round and see. He went round, opened the stable door, and next moment was struck full in the chest by what seemed to be a heavy missive hurled with tremendous force. It was Charles, who had leaped from the end of his chain to greet his master—Charles, alive and almost idiotic in his transports of uncouth affection. Edward felt the dog all over—to see if any bones were broken. Charles never winced. There was not a cut or a bruise on him! The two sat on the straw embracing for quite a long time.

"Yes, sir, seems quite himself, don't he?" said Robert. "Miss Davenant she brought him. Told me to tell you the dog come to himself quite sudden on the cart. Must have fainted, young miss said, and when he come to it was all she could do to hold him down. He seems to have come to quite sudden and all wild-like among their legs in the bottom of the cart till miss dragged him out—nearly upset the old lady right out of the cart, coming up sudden under her knees. Awful nasty she was about it. Said the dog must have been shamming. Thank you, sir. I'll drink your health and the dog's."

"Shamming, indeed!" said Edward to himself, and resented the cruel and silly aspersion. Yet, stay, was it really quite impossible that Charles, fearing that the same punishment might visit this last exploit as had followed his earlier outrages, had really shammed, to disarm a doting master? Edward put away the thought. It was impossible.

The main thing was that Charles was alive. But, after all, *was* that the main thing? Now that the dog was alive it suddenly ceased to be. The main thing was that he had not seen her that morning and that he must, somehow, see her again.

Somehow. But how? This gave him food for thought.

He went into his parlor and sat down—to think. But, try as he could, there seemed no way. Of course he could go next morning—of course he would go next morning—and every morning for a week. But if she hadn't come to-day, why should she come to-morrow or the next day, or the day after that?

Or the handkerchief. Wouldn't it be natural that he should call to return it and to thank them for taking care of the lifeless Charles, and apologize for that thoughtless animal's inconvenient and sudden change of attitude? Yes, that would have been natural if the girl had not blushed and if he had not turned scarlet.

He took out the handkerchief and spread it on the table—what silly little things girls' handkerchiefs were! Then he looked at it more closely. Then he took it to the window, stretched it tightly, and looked more closely than ever. Yes, there was something on it, something intended—not just the marks of the road. There were letters—pencil letters an inch or more long, very rough and straggling, but quite unmistakable—*Ce soir 12 heures*. At least, it might be 13, but, then, she wasn't an Italian.

The light of life blazed up, and the world suddenly became beautiful again. She had not forgotten—she had wished to come to meet him—something had prevented her coming in the morning. But to-night she would come. Twelve o'clock! A strange hour to choose. Bah! who was he to cavil at the hour she chose to set? How sweet and soft the handkerchief was!

V

LA MANCHE

THE bolts of the back door did not creak at all when, at twenty minutes to twelve, Edward Basingstoke let himself out. Tommy always saw to the bolts, for his own purposes, with a feather and a little salad oil.

The night was sweet and dark under the trees and in among the houses. In the village no lamp gleamed at any window. Beyond the village, the starshine and dew lent a gray shimmer to field and hedge, and the road lay before him like a pale ribbon. He crossed the meadow, climbed the wall, and dropped. The earth sounded dully under his feet, and twigs crackled as he moved. There was no other sound. She was not there. He dared not light a match to see his watch's face by. Perhaps he was early. Well, he could wait. He waited. He waited and waited and waited. He listened till his ears were full of the soft rustlings and movements which go to make up the silence of country night. He strained his eyes to see some movement in the gray park dotted with black trees. But all was still. It was very dark under the trees. And through all his listening he thought, thought. Did it do to trust to impulses —to instincts? Did it do, rather, to disregard them? A gipsy woman had said to him once, "Your first thoughts are straight—give yourself time to think twice and you'll think wrong." What he had felt that morning while he waited, vainly, for her to come had taught him that, fool as he might be for his pains, the feeling that possessed him was more like the love poets talked of than he would have believed any feeling of his could be. And, after all, love at first sight *was* possible—was it not the theme of half the romances in the world? He felt that at this, their second meeting, he must know whether he meant to advance or to retreat. Always when he had trusted his impulse his choice had been a wise one. But was a choice necessary now? His instincts told him that it was. This midnight meeting— planned by her and not by him—it was a meeting for "good-by." No girl would make an assignation at that hour just to tell a man that she intended to meet him again the next day. So he must know whether he meant to permit himself to be said good-by to. And he knew that he did not.

THE INCREDIBLE HONEYMOON

The day had been long, but it seemed to him that already the night had been longer than the day. Could he have mistaken the hour? No, it was certainly twelve—or thirteen. Then his heart leaped up. If it *had* been thirteen, that meant one o'clock. Perhaps it was not one yet. But he felt that he knew it to be at least three. Yet if it were three there would be the diffused faint illumination of dawn growing, growing. And there was no light at all but the changeless light of the stars. Again and again he thought he saw her, thought he heard her. And again and again only silence and solitude came to meet his thoughts.

When at last she did come he saw her very far off, and heard the rustle of her dress even before he saw her.

He would not go to meet her across the starlit space; that would be very dangerous. He stood where he was till she came into the shadow. Then he went toward her and said:

"At last!"

She drew a long breath. "Oh, I was so afraid you wouldn't come!"

"I was here at twelve," he said.

"So you got the handkerchief. I put thirteen because I thought if I put one—it was so difficult to write—and, of course, I couldn't look at it to see if it was readable. I wrote it under the driving-rug. Oh, suppose you hadn't got it!"

"I can't suppose it. What should I have done if I hadn't?"

"Oh," she said, "don't! Please don't. I thought you'd understand it was serious. I shouldn't have asked you to come in the middle of the night to talk nonsense as if we were at a dance."

"What's serious?" he said.

She said, "Everything," and her voice trembled.

He took her arm, and felt that she herself was trembling.

"Come and sit down," he said, comfortably, as one might speak to a child in trouble. "Come and sit down and tell me all about it."

They sat down on the log, and he pulled the dark cloak she wore more closely round her.

"Now," he said, "what's happened? Why didn't you come this morning?"

"I stayed too long the first time," she answered, "and met Aunt Loo as I went in. She asked me where I'd been. I said I'd been out to swim in the lake. That was quite true. That *was* why I had gone out. I've often done it. But, of course, my hair wasn't wet. She didn't say anything. But this morning when I came down she was sitting in the hall, waiting for me. She asked me if I was going bathing again, and I said, No, I was going to walk in the park. So she said, 'Charming idea. I'll come, too.'"

"And what did you say?"

"I said, 'Do,' of course. But it was awful. I was so afraid of her seeing you."

"Suppose she *had* chosen to walk that way."

"Yes, of course I thought of that. So *I* led the way and walked straight toward you. Then she thought whoever I was going to meet must be the other way. So she insisted on going the other way. I knew she would."

"That was subtle of you."

"No; it's only that she's stupid. It wouldn't have taken any one else in."

"So she was baffled."

"Yes, but she has instincts, though she's so stupid. She knew there was something up. And then when we met you—oh, I *am* so glad the dog's all right—when we met you I knew she thought you'd something to do with my being out so early in the morning, and then you blushed."

"If I did," he said, "I wasn't the only one."

"Oh, I know," she said, "but I don't suppose I should have if you hadn't. Though unjust suspicions like that are enough to make anybody blush. Yes, they were unjust because you had nothing to do with my going out the first time—why, I didn't even know there *was* a you. And

LA MANCHE

now all the fat's in the fire, and she's taking me to Ireland or Scotland to-morrow—she won't say which. And I couldn't bear to go and have you think I'd made an appointment and not kept it. It's so unbusiness-like to break appointments," she said.

"Does she suppose, then, that we—that I am—that you have—that I should—?"

"I don't know what she supposes. At least I do. But it's too silly. Now I've explained everything. Good-by. I'm glad you found the handkerchief—and I'm *awfully* glad about Charles."

"I didn't know you knew his name."

"The stableman said it when the dog ran between his knees and nearly knocked him down. It's a darling dog—but isn't it strong! Good-by!" She held out her hand. "Good-by," she said, again.

"No," said he, and held the hand.

There was a little pause.

"Say good-by," she said. "Indeed I must go."

"Why?" he asked, releasing the hand.

"I've said everything there was to say—I mean, what I came to say."

"There's a very great deal that you haven't told me. I don't understand. Who does your aunt think I am?"

"I would rather not tell you; you'd only laugh."

THE INCREDIBLE HONEYMOON

"But please tell me. I shouldn't."

A troubled silence answered him.

"Look here," he said, "I know there's a lot you haven't told me. Do tell me, and let me help you, if I can. You're worried and unhappy. I can hear it in your voice. Tell me. Things look different when you've put them into words. First of all, tell me who your aunt thought I was."

She sat down again with the air of definite decision. "Very well," she said, "if you will have it, she thought you were the piano-tuner. Why don't you laugh?"

"I'm not amused yet," he said. "What piano-tuner? And why should he—why should you—"

"The piano-tuner is a fence," she said, "and she thinks you're it."

"I don't understand a word you're saying."

"I don't care," she said, desperately. "I'll tell you the whole silly story and you can laugh, if you like. I sha'n't be offended. Last autumn father brought a man to lunch, quite a nice man—sensible, middle-aged, very well off—and next day he told me the man had proposed for me, and I'd better take him. He'd accepted for me."

"Good heavens!" said Edward, "I thought it was only in the *Family Herald* that such fathers existed."

LA MANCHE

"Laugh as much as you like," said she; "it's true, for all that. You see, I'd refused several before that. It's rather important for me to marry well—my father's not rich, and—"

"I see. Well?"

"Well, I wasn't going to. And when it came to this luncheon man I told you about there was a scene, and my father said was there any one else, and I said no; but he went on so frightfully and wouldn't believe me. So at last I told him."

"Told him what?"

"That there was some one."

"Yes?" His voice was only more gentle for the sudden sharp stab of disappointment which told him what hope it was that he had nursed.

"And then, of course, I wouldn't say who it was. And he sent for my aunts. Aunt Enid's worse than Aunt Loo. And they bothered and bothered. And at last I said it was the piano-tuner. I don't know how I could have. Father turned him off, of course, poor wretch, and they brought me down here to come to my senses. Aunt Loo never saw the miserable piano-tuner, and she thinks you're him. So now you know. And that's why they're taking me away from here. They think the piano-tuner is pursuing me. I believe Aunt Loo thinks you trained the dog to bark at horses so as to get a chance to speak to me."

THE INCREDIBLE HONEYMOON

"Do you care much for your father?" he asked, "or for any of them?"

"It's a horrid thing to say," she answered, "but I don't. The only one I care for's Aunt Alice—she's an invalid and a darling. Father thinks about nothing but bridge and races, and Aunt Loo's all golf and horses, and Aunt Enid's a social reformer. I hate them all. And I've never been anywhere or seen anything. I'm not allowed to write to any one. And they don't have any one here at all, and I'm not to see a single soul till I've come to my senses, as they call it. And that's why I was so glad to talk to you yesterday."

"I see," he said, very kindly. "Now what can I do for you? Where's the other man? Can't I post a letter to him or something? Why doesn't he come and rescue you?"

"What other man?" she asked.

"The man you're fond of. The man whose name you wouldn't tell them."

"Oh," she said, lightly, and just as though it didn't matter. "There isn't any other man."

"There isn't?" he echoed, joyously.

"No, of course not. I just made him up—and then I called him the piano-tuner."

"Then," he said, "forgive me for asking, but I must be quite sure—you don't care for any man at all?"

LA MANCHE

"Of course I don't," she answered, resentfully, "I shouldn't go about caring about any one who didn't care for me—and if any one cared for me and I cared for him, of course we should run away with each other at once."

"I see," said Mr. Basingstoke, slowly and distinctly. "Then if there isn't any one else I suggest that you run away with me."

It was fully half a minute before she spoke. Then she said: "I don't blame you. I deserve it for asking you to meet me and coming out like this. But I thought you were different."

"Deserve what?"

"To be insulted and humiliated. To be made a jest of."

"It seems to me that my offer is no more insulting or humiliating than any of your other offers. I like you very much. I think you like me. And I believe we should suit each other very well. Don't be angry. I'm perfectly serious. Don't speak for a minute. Listen. I've just come into some money, and I'm going about the country, seeing places and people. I'm just a tramp, as I told you. Come and be a tramp, too. We'll go anywhere you like. We'll take the map and you shall put your finger on any place you think you'd like to see, and we'll go straight off to it, by rail or motor, or in a cart, or a caravan, if you'd like it.

Caravans must be charming. To go wherever you like, stop when you like—go on when you like. Come with me. I don't believe you'd ever regret it. And I know I never should."

"I believe you're serious," she said, half incredulously.

"Of course I am. It's a way out of all your troubles."

"I couldn't," she said, earnestly, "marry any one I wasn't very fond of. And one can't be fond of a person one's only seen twice."

"Can't you?" he said, a little sadly.

"No," she answered. "I think it's very fine of you to offer me this—just to get me out of a bother. And I'm sorry I thought you were being horrid. I'll tell you something. I've always thought that even if I cared very much for some one I should be almost afraid to marry him unless I knew him very, very well. Girls do make such frightful mistakes. You ought to see a man every day for a year, and then, perhaps, you'd know if you could really bear to live with him all your life."

Instead of answering her directly, he said: "You would love the life in the caravan. Think of the camp—making a fire of sticks and cooking your supper under the stars, and the great moonlit nights, and sleeping in pine woods and waking in the dawn and curling yourself up in your blanket and going to sleep again till I shouted out that the fire was alight and breakfast nearly ready."

"I wish I could come with you without having to be married."

"Come, then," he said. "Come on any terms. I'll take you as a sister if I'm not to take you as a wife."

"Do you mean it? Really?" she said. "Oh, why shouldn't I? I believe you would take me—and I should be perfectly free then. I've got a little money of my own that my godmother left me. I was twenty-one the other day. I don't get it, of course. My father says it costs that to keep me. But if I were to run away he would have to give it to me, wouldn't he? And then I could pay you back what you spent on me. Oh, I wish I could. Will you really take me?"

But he had had time to think. "No," he said, "on reflection, I don't think I will."

But she did not hear him, for as he spoke she spoke, too. "Hush!" she said. "Look — look there."

Across the park, near the house, lights were moving.

"They're looking for me," she gasped. "They've found out that I'm away. Oh, what shall I do? Aunt Loo will never be decent to me again. What *shall* I do?"

"Come with me," he said, strongly. "I'll take care of you. Come."

He took her hand. "I swear by God," he said, "that everything shall be as you choose. Only come now—come away from these people. You're twenty-one. You're your own mistress. Let me help you to get free from all this stuffy, stupid tyranny."

"You won't make me marry you?" she asked.

"I can't make you do anything," he said. "But if you're coming, it must be now."

"Come, then," she said, making for the ladder.

VI

CROW'S NEST

HE had brought a ball of string in his pocket, this time, and he was glad to know he could lower the ladder by it—for the thud of a falling ladder would sound far in the night stillness. From the top of the wall he held the ladder while she mounted.

"Sit here a moment," he said, "while I get rid of the ladder." He lowered it gently, drew the string up, leaped to the ground outside the wall, and held up his hands to her.

"Jump," he whispered. "I'll catch you."

But even as he spoke she had turned and was hanging by her hands. He let her do it her own way. She dropped expertly, landing with a little rebound. He was glad he had not tried to catch her. It would have been a poor beginning to their comradeship if he had, at the very outset, shown doubts of her competence to do anything she set out to do.

They stood under the wall very near together.

"What are you going to do?" she said.

"I must get a car and take you away. Are you afraid to be left alone for a couple of hours?"

"I—I don't think so," she said. "But where? Did you notice the lights as you got over the wall?"

"Yes; they were still near the house."

The two were walking side by side along the road now.

"If you were any ordinary girl I should be afraid to leave you to think things over—for fear you should think you'd been rash or silly or something—and worry yourself about all sorts of nonsense, and perhaps end in bolting back to your hutch before I could come back to you. But since it's you—let's cut across the downs here—we'll keep close to the edge of the wood."

Their feet now trod the soft grass.

"How sensible of you to wear a dark cloak," he said.

"Yes," she said, "a really romantic young lady in distress would have come in white muslin and blue ribbons, wouldn't she?"

He glowed to the courage that let her jest at such a moment.

"Where am I to wait?" she asked.

"There's an old farm-house not far away," he

CROW'S NEST

said. "If you don't mind waiting there. Could you?"

"Who lives there?"

"Nobody. I happen to have the key. I was looking at it yesterday. It's not furnished, but I noticed some straw and packing-cases. I could rig you up some sort of lounge, but don't do it if you're afraid. If you're afraid to be left to yourself we'll walk together to Eastbourne. But if we do we're much more likely to be caught."

"I'm not in the least afraid. Why should I be?" she said, and they toiled up the hill among the furze bushes in the still starlight.

"What they'll do," she said, presently, "when they're sure I'm not in the park, is to go down to your inn and see if you're there."

"Yes," he said, "I'm counting on that. That's why I said two or three hours. You see, I must be there when they do come, and the minute they're gone I'll go for the motor. Look here—I've got some chocolate that I got for a kiddy to-day; luckily, I forgot to give it to him; and here are some matches, only don't strike them if you can help it. Now, stick to it."

They went on in silence; half-way up the hill he took her arm to help her. Then, over the crest of the hill, in a hollow of the downs there was the dark-spread blot of house and farm build-

THE INCREDIBLE HONEYMOON

ings. They went down the road. Nothing stirred—only as they neared the farm-yard a horse in the stable rattled his halter against the manger and they heard his hoofs moving on the cobbled floor of his stall. They stood listening. No, all was still.

"Give me your hand," he said, and led her round to the side of the house. The key grated a little as he turned it in the lock. He threw back the door.

"This is the kitchen," he said. "Stand just inside and I'll make a nest for you. I know exactly where to lay my hands on the straw."

There was rustling in the darkness and a sound of boards grating on bricks. She stood at the door and waited.

"Ready," he said.

"They'll find me," she said. "We shall never get away."

"Trust me for that," said he.

"I must have been mad to come," he heard through the darkness.

"We're all mad once in our lives," he said, cheerfully. "Now roll yourself in your cloak. Give me your hands—so." He led her to the straw nest he had made, and lowered her to it.

"Do you wish you hadn't come?" he asked.

"I don't know," she said.

CROW'S NEST

"I hope to Heaven I haven't misjudged you," he said, with the first trace of anxiety she had yet heard in his voice. "If you should be the kind of girl who's afraid of the dark—"

The straw rustled as she curled herself more comfortably in her nest.

"I'm not afraid," she said.

"Look here," said he, "here's my match-box, but don't strike a light among the straw. The door into the house is locked and the key's on this side of the door. Can you come to the back door and lock it after me, and then find your way back to your nest?"

"Yes," she said, and felt her way past the big copper to the door.

"Sure you're not frightened?"

"Quite," said she.

"Then I'll go," said he, and went.

She locked the door and crept back to the straw. He waited till its crackling told him that she had found her way back to her couch. Then he started for Jevington.

And as he went he told himself that she was right. She had been mad to come, and he had been mad to let her come. But there was no going back now.

There was no looking back, even. From the brow of the hill the road was down-hill all the way, and he ran, his rubber shoes patting almost noiselessly in the dust. At his inn the bolt yielded to his knife-point's pressure, the well-oiled lock let him in without a murmur, the stairs hardly creaked more than stairs can creak in their dark solitudes when we lie awake and listen to them and wonder. . . . The night was as silent as a thought, and when at last the silence was shattered by the clatter of hoofs and the jangle of harness, Mr. Basingstoke's head turned a little on his pillow, not restlessly.

He heard the clanging bell echo in the flagged passage; heard through the plaster walls the heavy awakening of his host, the scrape of a match, the hasty, blundering toilet; heard the big bar dropped from the front door; voices—the groom's voice, the host's voice, the aunt's voice.

Then heavy steps on the stairs and a knock at his door.

"Very sorry to disturb you, sir," came the muffled tones through the door, almost cringingly apologetic, "but could you get up, sir, just for a minute? Miss Davenant from the Hall wants a word with you—about your dawg, sir, as I understand. If you could oblige, sir—very inconvenient, I know, sir, but the Hall is very highly thought of in the village, sir."

CROW'S NEST

"What on earth—?" said Mr. Basingstoke, very loudly, and got out of bed. "I'll dress and come down," he said.

He did dress, to the accompaniment of voices below—replaced, that is, the collar, tie, and boots he had taken off—and then he began to pack, his mind busy with the phrases in which he would explain that a house in which these nocturnal disturbances occurred was not fit for the sojourning of . . . No, hang it all, that would not be fair to the landlord—he must find some other tale.

When he had kept the lady waiting as long as he thought a man might have kept her who had really a toilet to make, he went slowly down. Voices sounded in the parlor, and a slab of light from its door lay across the sanded passage.

He went in; the landlord went out, closing the door almost too discreetly.

Mr. Basingstoke and the aunt looked at each other. She was very upright and wore brown gloves and a brown, boat-shaped hat with an aggressive quill.

"You *are* here, then?" she said.

"Where else, madam?" said Mr. Basingstoke.

"I should like you," said the aunt, deliberately, "to be somewhere else within the next hour. I will make it worth your while."

"Thank you," Edward murmured.

THE INCREDIBLE HONEYMOON

"I think I ought to tell you," said she, "that I saw through that business of the dog. He was well trained, I admit. But I can't have my niece annoyed in this way."

"The lady must certainly not be annoyed," said Edward, with feeling.

"I came to-night to see if you were here . . ."

"It is an unusual hour for a call," said Edward, "but I am proportionally honored."

"—to see if you were here, and, if you were, to tell you that my niece is not."

Edward cast a puzzled eye around the crowded parlor. "No," he said. "No."

"I mean," Miss Davenant went on, "that my niece has left this neighborhood and will not return while you are here; so you are wasting your time and trouble."

"*I* see," said Edward, helpfully.

"You will gain nothing by this attitude," said Miss Davenant. "If you will consent to leave Jevington to-night I will give you twenty pounds."

"Twenty pounds!" he repeated, softly.

"Yes, twenty pounds, on condition that you promise not to molest this defenseless girl."

"Put up your money, madam," said Edward Basingstoke, with a noble gesture copied from the best theatrical models, "and dry your eyes. Never shall it be said that Edward Basingstoke was deaf to the voice of a lady in distress. Lay your commands on me, and be assured that, for me, to hear is to obey."

"You are very impertinent, young man," Miss Davenant told him, "and you won't do yourself any good by talking like a book. Clear out of this to-night, and I'll give you twenty pounds. Stay, and take the consequences."

"Meaning—?"

"Well, stay if you like. You won't see her. She won't return to Jevington till you're gone. So I tell you you'd better accept my offer and go."

"Accept your offer and go," repeated Edward.

"Twenty pounds," said the lady, persuasively.

"Tempt me not!" said Edward. "To a man in my position . . ."

"Exactly."

"Nay," said Edward, "there are chords even in a piano-tuner's breast—chords which, too roughly touched, will turn and rend the smiter."

"Good gracious!" said Miss Davenant, "I believe the man's insane."

"Withdraw that harsh expression," he pleaded. And then, without warning, the situation ceased to amuse him. Here he was, swimming in the deep, smooth waters of diplomacy, and suddenly diplomacy seemed a sticky medium. He would have liked Miss Davenant to be a man—a man in green-silk Georgian coat and buckled shoes; himself also gloriously Georgian, in murray-colored cut velvet, with Mechlin at wrists and throat. Then they could have betaken themselves to the bowling-green and fought it out with ringing rapiers, by the light of the lantern held in the landlord's trembling fingers. Or at dawn, in the meadow the red wall bounded, there could have been measured pacings—a dropped handkerchief, two white puffs drifting away on the chill, sweet air, and Edward Basingstoke could have handed his smoking pistol to his second and mounted his horse—Black Belial—and so away to his lady, leaving his adversary wounded slightly ("winged," of course, was the word). Thus honor would have been satisfied, and Edward well in the lime-light. But in this little box of an overfurnished room, by the light of an ill-trimmed paraffin-lamp, to rag an anxious aunt . . . He withdrew himself slowly from diplomacy—tried to find an inch or two of dry truth to stand on.

"Well, why don't you say something?" asked the anxious aunt.

"I will," said Mr. Basingstoke. "Madam, I have to ask your pardon for an unpardonable liberty. I have deceived you. I am not what you think. I am not a piano-tuner, but an engineer."

"But you said you were. . . ."

"Pardon me. I said there were chords in the breasts of piano-tuners."

"But if you aren't, how did you know there was one?"

This *riposte* he had not anticipated. Frankness had its drawbacks—so small a measure of it as he had allowed himself. He leaped headlong into diplomacy again.

"Look back on what you have said, not only to me, but to others," he said, solemnly, and saw that the chance shot had gone home. "Now," he said, "don't let us prolong an interview which cannot but be painful to us both. I am not the piano-tuner for whom you take me. You are a complete stranger to me. The only link that binds us is the fact that your horse ran over my dog and that you bore the apparently lifeless body home for me. Yet if you wish me to leave the neighborhood, I will leave it. In fact, I was going in any case," he added, struggling against diplomacy.

Miss Davenant looked at him. "You're speaking the truth," she said; "you're not the piano-tuner. But you got as red as fire yesterday. So did my niece. What was that for?"

"I cannot explain my complicated color-scheme," said Edward, "without diagrams and a

THE INCREDIBLE HONEYMOON

magic-lantern. And as for your niece, I can lay my hand on my heart and say that the light of declining day never illumined that face for me till the moment when it also illumined yours."

"Are you deceiving me?" Miss Davenant asked, weakly, and Edward answered:

"Yes, I am; but not in the way you think. We all have our secrets, but mine are not the secrets of the piano-tuner."

Some one sneezed in the passage outside.

"Our host has been eavesdropping," said Edward, softly.

"Well, if he doesn't make more of this conversation than I do, he won't make much," said Miss Davenant. "I don't trust you."

"That would make it all the easier for me to deceive you," said Edward, "if I sought to deceive."

"You've got too much language for me," said Miss Davenant. "If you're not the man, I apologize."

"Don't mention it," said Edward.

"If you are, I don't wonder so much at what happened in London. Good night. Sorry to have disturbed you."

"Don't you think," said Edward, "that you might as well tell me why you *did* disturb me?"

"I thought you were the piano-tuner," she said;

"you knew that perfectly well. And I don't want piano-tuners hanging round Jevington. I'm sorry I offered the money. I ought to have seen."

"Not at all," said Mr. Basingstoke, "and, since my presence here annoys you, know that by this time to-morrow I shall be far away."

"There's one thing more," said Miss Davenant. But Mr. Basingstoke was never to know what that one thing was, for at the instant a wild shriek rang through the quiet night, there was a scuffle outside, hoarse voices in anger and pain, the door burst open, and Miss Davenant's groom staggered in.

"Beg pardon, ma'am"—he still remembered his station, and it was thus he affirmed it—"beg pardon, ma'am, but this 'ere dawg—"

It was too true. Charles, perhaps conscious of his master's presence in the parlor, had slipped his collar, scratched a hole under the stable door, and, finding the groom and the landlord in the passage, barring his entrance, had bitten the groom's trousers leg. It hung, gaping, from knee to ankle—with Charles still attached. Charles's master choked the dog off, but confidential conversation was at an end, even when a sovereign had slipped from his hand to the groom's.

"Seems the young lady's missing," said the host, when the dog-cart had rattled up the street.

THE INCREDIBLE HONEYMOON

"Indeed!" said Edward. "Well, I think I also shall retreat. Will it inconvenience you if I leave my traps to be sent on? I shall walk into Seaford and catch the early train."

"It wasn't my fault the lady come, sir," said the landlord, sulky but deferential.

"I know it," said the guest, "and I am not leaving because of her coming. I should have left in any case. But it is a fine night, I have a fancy for a walk, and it does not seem worth while to go to bed again. If you will kindly take this, pay your bill out of it, and divide the remainder between Robert and Gladys, I shall be very much obliged. I've been very comfortable here and I shall certainly come again."

He pressed a five-pound note into the landlord's hand, and before that bewildered one could think of anything more urgent than the commonplaces which begin, "I'm sure, sir," or, "I shouldn't like to think," he and Charles had turned their backs on the Five Bells, and the landlord was staring after them. The round, white back of Charles showed for quite a long time through the darkness. Slowly he drew the bolts, put out the lights, and went back to bed.

"It's a rum go," he told his wife, after he had told her all he had heard and overheard, "a most peculiar rum go. But he's a gentleman, he is, whichever way you look at it. Miss up at the Hall might do a jolly sight worse, if you ask me. Shouldn't wonder, come to think of it, if she ain't waiting for him around the corner, as it is."

"He's the kind of gentleman a girl *would* wait around the corner for," said the landlady. "It's his eyes, partly, I think. And he's got such a kind look. But if she is—waiting round the corner, I mean, like what you said—he *have* got a face to go on like what he did to Miss Davenant."

"Yes," said the landlord, blowing out the candle, "he *have* got a face, whichever way you look at it."

It was bright daylight when a motor—one of the strong, fierce kind, no wretched taxicab, but a private motor of obvious speed and spirit—blundered over the shoulder of the downs down the rutty road to Crow's Nest Farm.

Mr. Basingstoke, happy to his finger-tips as well as to the inmost recesses of the mind in his consciousness of results achieved and difficulties overcome, slipped from the throbbing motor and went quickly around to the back door, Charles with him, straining at the lead. The path that led to the door had its bricks outlined with green grass, a house-leek spread its rosettes on the sloping lichened tiles of the roof, and in the corner of the window the toad-flax flaunted its little helmets of orange and sulphur-color. He tapped gently on the door. Nothing from within answered him—no voice, no movement, no creak of board, no rustle of straw, no click of little heels on the floor of stone. She might be asleep—must be. He knocked again, and still silence answered him. Then a wave of possibilities and impossibilities rose suddenly and swept against Mr. Basingstoke's heart. So sudden was it, and so strong was it, that for a moment he felt the tremor of a physical nausea. He put his hand to the latch, meaning to try with his shoulder the forcing of the lock. But the door was not locked. The latch clicked, yielding to his hand, and the door opened into the kitchen, with its wide old chimneyplace, big mantel-shelf, its oven and pump, its brewing-copper and its washing-copper, its litter of packing-cases and straw, and the little nest he had made for her between the copper and the big barrel. The soft, diffused daylight showed him every corner, and Charles sniffing, as it seemed, every corner at once. He crossed over and tried the door that led to the house. But he knew, before his hand found it unyielding, that it had not been unlocked since last he saw it. He knew, quite surely, that the lady was not there. There was no sign or trace of her, save the rounded nest where she must have snuggled for at least a part of the night that he had spent in such strenuous diplomacy, such ardent organization, for her sake. No other trace of her . . . yes, on the flap-table by the window his match-box, set as weight to keep in its place a handkerchief. It was own sister to the little one his pocket still held—and, as he took it up, exhaled the same faint, delicate fragrance. He read it, Charles snuffling and burrowing in the straw at his feet. On it a few words were written, some illegible, but these few plain:

I will write to General Post-Office, London.

There are no words for the thoughts of the baffled adventurer as he locked the door and walked around the farm to the waiting motor. His only word on the way was to Charles, and it calmed, for an instant, even that restless spirit.

"London," he said to his chauffeur. "My friend isn't coming," and he and Charles tumbled into the car together.

A line of faces drawn up against a long fence watched his departure with mild curiosity. Twenty or thirty calves and their rustic attendant saw him go. The chauffeur looked again at the house's blank windows and echoed the landlord's words.

"Rum go!" he said to himself. "Most extraordinary rum go."

VII

TUNBRIDGE WELLS

AN earnest and prolonged struggle with Charles now occupied Mr. Basingstoke. Charles was determined to stand on the seat with his paws on the side of the car, to look out and to be in readiness to leap out should any passing object offer a more than trivial appeal. His master was determined that Charles should lie on the mat in the bottom of the car, and, what is more, that he should lie there quietly. The discussion became animated and ended in blows. It was just at the crisis of the affair, when Edward had lightly smitten the hard, bullet head and Charles was protesting with screams as piercing as those of a locomotive in distress, that the car wheeled into the highroad and narrowly missed a dog-cart coming up from Seaford. As they passed, Edward's hand went to his hat, for the driver of the dog-cart was Miss Davenant.

Charles, partially released, leaped toward the

lady, only to hang by his chain over the edge of the car. By the time he had been hauled in again and cuffed into comparative quiescence Miss Davenant was left far behind, a little, gesticulating figure against the horizon. Her gestures seemed to Edward to be gestures of recall. But he disregarded them. It was not till later that he regretted this.

A final struggle with Charles ended in victory, not because Edward had enforced his will on that strong and strenuous nature, but because Charles was now exhausted and personally inclined to surrender. He lay at last on the floor of the car, his jaws open in a wide, white-toothed smile, and his pink tongue palpitating to his panting breaths. Edward sat very upright, his hands between his knees, holding the shortened chain of Charles. Mile after mile of the smooth down country slipped past, the car had whirled down the narrow, tree-bordered road into Alfreston, past the old church and the thirteenth-century, half-timbered Clergy House, where three little girls in green pinafores were seeking to coerce a reluctant goat along to Polegate and across the railway lines, and still Mr. Basingstoke never moved. His mind alone was alive, and of his body he was no longer conscious. He thought and thought and thought. Why had she left the farm? Had she been frightened? Had she been captured? Where had she gone? And why? And behind all these questions was a background of something too vague and yet too complicated to be called regret—or something which, translated into words, might have gone something like this:

"Adventures to the adventurous. And three days ago the world was before me. I had set out for adventures and I found nothing more agitating than the pleasant pleasing of one little child. Then suddenly the adventure happened. And now no more charming wanderings, no more aimless saunterings in this pleasant, green world, but rush and worry and hurry and dust, uncertainty, anxiety, . . . the whole pretty dream of the adventurer shattered by the reality of the adventure."

Suddenly, and without meaning to do it, he had mortgaged his future to a stranger. The stranger had fled and he was—well, not pursuing, but going to the place she had named as that from which he might gain a clue and take up the pursuit. It was not exactly regret, but Mr. Basingstoke found himself almost wishing that time could move backward and set him in the meadow where the red wall was, and give him once more the chance to fly or not to fly his aeroplane. Perhaps if he had the choice he would not fly it. But all this was among the shadows at the back of his mind. In the foreground was the small, insistent cycle of questions: Why had she left the farm? Had she been frightened? Had she been captured? Where had she gone? When? How? Why?

It was not till the car was slipping through Crowborough, that paradise of villa-dwellers who have "done well in business," that the thought came to him, had she, after all, gone back to her aunt? Had she thought better of it, and just gone humbly back with confession and submission in both hands? It was then that he remembered that Miss Davenant had seemed to signal . . . perhaps she had some errand to him . . . perhaps submission had been given as the price of a farewell message, aunt-borne, to meet him at the farm? Mr. Basingstoke was not subject to attacks of indecision, but now for a moment he wavered. Then imagination showed him himself on the door-step of the Hall asking for Miss Davenant, and Miss Davenant receiving or not receiving him—in either case he himself cutting a figure which he could not for a moment admire. Common sense reinforced imagination. The handkerchief said General Post-Office. It could only have said that if the handkerchief's owner meant him to go to the General Post-Office. If the handkerchief's owner had meant him to go back to the Hall, the handkerchief could just as easily have said the Hall. He went back to his questionings, and the car drew near Tunbridge Wells.

Charles, exhausted by the morning's combat, had slept heavily, but now he roused himself to take the rôle of Arbiter of Destinies. He roused himself, sat up, snuffled and blew, and then, with wide smile and lolling tongue, proclaimed himself to be that pitiable and suffering creature, a bull-terrier dying of thirst. In vain Edward sought to calm him; he insisted that he was, and that he had a right to be, thirsty. His insistence affected his master. Edward became aware that he, also, was thirsty; more, was hungry. His watch showed him that the chauffeur had every right to consider himself an ill-used man. A bright-faced hotel whose windows were underlined with marguerites and pink geraniums beckoned attractively.

"After all, one must live," said Edward, and breathed an order. The car drew up in front of the White Horse.

Another car was there—unattended—a very nice car. Edward wished it had been his. It had all those charms which his own hired one lacked, and his experienced eye dwelt fondly on those charms.

"Get yourself something to eat," he said to the chauffeur. Charles, straining toward the horse-trough, seemed anxious to prove that his thirst had not been simulated. Edward indulged him. Arrived at the wet granite, however, Charles lapped a tongueful or two, as it were out of politeness and merely to oblige, and then looked up at his master expressively. "You have sadly misunderstood me," he seemed to say. "What I wanted was breakfast," adding, reproachfully, "You will remember that there has been none to-day."

He dragged his master to the hotel door, where they passed in under hanging-baskets of pink and white flowers, and in a coffee-room adorned with trophies of the chase Edward ordered luncheon for himself and biscuits for Charles. Now mark the vagaries of Destiny: Charles, impatient for the biscuits, dragged his chain about the coffee-room, empty at this hour of all but himself and his master; he upset the tongs and the shovel and brought them clattering to the fender. Edward replaced them in their stands. Then Charles put his feet in an antimacassar and dragged it to the floor. After this he went to the writing-table under the wire blind in the middle window and snuffled curiously in the waste-paper basket, upsetting it almost without an effort, and a litter of letters and envelopes and torn circulars was discharged.

Edward, hastening to repair these ravages,

THE INCREDIBLE HONEYMOON

scooped the torn fragments in his hands—and on the very top, fronting him, was an envelope bearing his own name—Basingstoke.

"—Basingstoke," the envelope said plainly, adding as an incomplete afterthought, "General Post-O"— and there ending. The handwriting was, like Hypatia's, graceful and self-conscious. That is to say, it was legible, clear, and the letters were shaped by design and not by accident. He never doubted for an instant whose hand it was that had written those words. He went through the waste-paper basket's other contents for more of that handwriting. There was not a scrap. The waiter, coming in with accessories to the still-withheld luncheon, stared at him.

"Something thrown away by mistake," he said, and pursued the search. No—nothing.

But that she had been here was plain; that she still might be here was possible. She must have come by train or by motor—what motor? Train from what station? He went out into the hall to question the highly coiffured young lady whom he had noticed as he came in, the lady who sits in the glass cage where the keys are kept, and enters your name in the book when you engage your room. The cage was empty, the hall was empty. On the hall-table's dark mahogany lay a shining salver, and on the salver lay a few letters. He picked them up. The one on the top was addressed fully—to

> Mr. Basingstoke,
>   General Post-Office,
>   London.

The one below was addressed to—

> Miss Davenant,
>   The Hall,
>   Jevington,
>   Sussex.

Edward glanced round; he was still alone. He put the letters in his pocket and went back to the coffee-room. Charles's attentions had been directed, in his absence, to the waiter, who had thus been detained from his duties.

"Any one else lunching here to-day?" he asked, restraining Charles.

"Mostly over by now, sir," said the waiter. "That dog—dangerous, ain't he, sir?"

"Not a bit," said Edward; "he only took a fancy to you."

"Wouldn't let me pass—like," said the waiter.

"Only his play," said Edward. "He merely wants his dinner. You've been rather a long time bringing his biscuits. I expect he thought you'd got them in your pocket."

THE INCREDIBLE HONEYMOON

"Sorry, sir," the waiter said, and explained that, being single-handed at that hour, he had had to attend to the other party's lunch, "in the garden, sir," he added, "though why the garden when everything's nice and ready in here—to say nothing of earwigs in your glass, and beetles, and everything to be carried half a mile—" He ceased abruptly.

"I should like to see the garden," said Edward, "while I'm waiting."

"Lunch ready directly, sir," said the waiter. "Hardly worth while to have it out there now, sir—"

"Which way?" Edward asked, and was told. He went through the hall, under a vine-covered trellis, and the garden blazed before him—a really charming garden, all green and red and yellow; beyond the lawn was an arbor with a light network of hops above it. In that arbor was a white-spread table. There was also movement; people were seated at the table.

Edward stood in the sunshine between two tall vases overflowing with nasturtiums and lobelias and opened his letter.

"Good-by," it said, "and thank you a thousand times. I shall never forget your kindness. But when I had time to think I saw that it wasn't fair to you. But you showed me the way out of the trap. And, now I am free, I can go on by myself. I don't want to drag you into any bother there may be. It would be a poor return for your kindness."

Initials followed—"K. D."

Mr. Basingstoke dragged at the chain of Charles, who was already gardening industrially in a bed of begonias, and walked straight to the arbor. It could not, of course, be she whose skirt he saw through the dappled screen of leaf and shadow. The waiter would never have called her a "party" —still, one might as well make sure before one began to make inquiries of the hotel people. So he walked around to the arbor's entrance and looked in. A man and woman were seated with a little table between them; coffee, peaches, and red wine announced the meal's completion. The man was a stranger. The woman was Herself. She raised her eyes as he darkened the doorway and they stared at each other for an instant in a stricken silence. It was a terrible moment for Edward. Recognition might be the falsest of false steps. On the other hand. . . . The question was, of course, one that must be left to her to decide. The man with her was too young to be her father; he might, of course, be an uncle or a brother. Untimely recognition on Edward's part might mean the end of all things. It was only a moment, though an incredibly long one. Then she smiled.

"Oh," she said, "here you are!" And before Edward had time to wonder what his next move was, or was expected to be, she had turned to her companion and said, "This is my brother; he will be able to thank you better than I can for your kindness."

The stranger, a strongly built man with blue eyes and a red neck, looked from one to the other. It may have been Mr. Basingstoke's fancy, but to him it seemed that the stranger's glance was seeking that elusive thing, a family likeness. His look said that he did not find it. His voice said,

"Not at all. Delighted to have been of the slightest service."

"What's happened?" asked Edward, feeling his way.

"Why," she hastened to explain, "when you didn't turn up I started to walk, and I didn't put on sensible shoes." A foot shod in a worn satin slipper crept out to point the confession and vanished at once. "And I sat down on a heap of stones to wait for you. And then this gentleman came by and offered me a lift. And I couldn't think what had become of you—and you know how important it was to get to London—so, of course, I was most grateful. And then something went wrong with the motor, so we stopped here for lunch—and I can't think how you found me—but I'm so glad you did. And all's well that ends well."

Edward felt that he was scowling, and all his efforts could not smooth out the scowl. She was patting Charles and looking at Charles's master.

"We are very much indebted to you, sir," said Edward, coldly.

"Nothing, I assure you," said the gentleman with the red neck. "Only too happy to be of service to Miss—er—"

"Basingstoke," said Edward, and saw in her eyes that he had not done the right thing. "I suppose you forgot to write to Aunt Emily and Uncle James," he said, seeking to retrieve the last move.

"Indeed I didn't," she said, with plain relief. "I wrote directly I got here, and gave them to the waiter to post."

Another silence longer than the first was broken by the waiter, who came to announce that the gentleman's lunch was ready in the coffee-room. The other gentleman—red-necked—asked for his bill.

While the waiter was gone for it, Edward put a sovereign on the table. "For my sister's share," he said.

THE INCREDIBLE HONEYMOON

The red-necked gentleman protested.

"You know," she said, in a low voice, "I said I should pay my share."

The red-necked gentleman rose. "I will tell them," he said, "to make out your bill separately. And now, if I cannot be of any further service to you, I think I'll be getting on. Good day to you."

"Good day," said Edward, "and thank you for your kindness to my sister."

"Good-by," said she, "and thank you a thousand times." She held out her hand. He bowed over it and went away through the sunlit garden, resentment obvious in every line of his back.

Neither Edward nor the girl spoke. There was no sound in the arbor save the convulsive gulpings of Charles absorbing the sponge fingers which she absently offered him from among the scattered dessert.

It was she who broke the silence. "I did write," she said.

"Yes. I got the letter." He laid it and Miss Davenant's on the table. "What does it mean?"

"What it says—"

"You won't let *me* help you—but you let that man, right enough."

"What was I to do? The important thing was to get away."

"What tale did you tell that man?"

TUNBRIDGE WELLS

"The truth."

He scowled with bitter skepticism.

"I did. Except that you're not my brother. I told him I'd missed you and that I'd got to get to London to-day as early as I could. And he was awfully nice and kind."

"I can well believe it."

"*Nice* and kind," she repeated, with emphasis. "And you were most horrid to him. And I do think you're unkind—"

"I don't mean to be," said Edward, "and it's not my province to be horrid and unkind to you, any more than it is to be nice and kind. In this letter you say good-by. Am I to understand that you mean good-by—that I am to leave you, here —now?"

She did not answer, and there was that in her silence which laid a healing touch on his hurt vanity.

"If my manner doesn't please you," he went on, "do remember that you have brought a fairly solid Spanish castle about my ears and that I am still a little bewildered and bruised."

"I'm sorry," she said, "but I didn't think."

"You see," he went on, "I thought I'd found a girl who wasn't just like other girls. . . ."

"I'm afraid I am," she said—"just."

"I thought that you were brave and truthful

THE INCREDIBLE HONEYMOON

and strong—and that you trusted me; and then I find you haven't the courage to stick to the way we planned; you haven't even the courage to wait for me and tell me you've changed your mind. You bolt off like a frightened rabbit and make friends with the first bounder who comes along. I was a fool to think I could help you. You don't need my help. Anybody else can help you just as well. Good-by—"

"Good-by," she said, not looking up. And he perceived that she was weeping. Also that he was no longer angry.

"Don't!" he said, "oh, don't! Do forgive me. I don't know what I've said. But I didn't mean it, whatever it was, if it's hurt you. I'll do just what you say. Shall I call that chap back?"

She shook her head and hid her face in her hands.

"Forgive me," he said again. "Oh, don't cry! I'm not worth it. Nothing's worth it. Charles, you brute, lie down." For Charles, in eager sympathy with beauty in distress, was leaping up in vain efforts to find and kiss the hidden face.

"Don't scold him," she said. "I like him." And Edward could have worshiped her for the words. "And, oh," she said, after a minute, "don't scold me, either! I'm so frightfully tired and everything's been so hateful. I thought you'd understand, and that if you cared to find me, you would."

"How could I? You sent no address."

"I did. On the handkerchief. . . . But I suppose you couldn't read it."

"And still," he said, but quite gently now, "I don't understand—"

"Don't you? Don't you see, I thought when you'd had time to think it over you'd be sorry and wish yourself well out of it, and yet feel obliged to go on. And I thought how horrid for you. And how much easier for you if you just thought I'd changed my mind. And then I set out to walk to Seaford and take the train. And then my shoes gave out, and I was so awfully afraid of aunt coming along that way, so that when Mr. Schultz came along it seemed a perfect godsend."

"So that's his foreign and unhappy name?" said Edward. "How did he come to tell it to you?"

"He had to," she said. "I borrowed ten pounds of him. I couldn't have gone to Claridge's without money, you know."

"Why Claridge's?"

"It's the only hotel that I know. And I had to have his name and address to send it back."

"May I send it back this afternoon?" Edward asked.

THE INCREDIBLE HONEYMOON

"Yes—"

"And you take back all you said in the letter? You don't mean it?"

"Not if you didn't want me to."

"And it wasn't really only because you thought I . . ."

"Of course. At least . . ."

"Well, then," said Mr. Basingstoke, happily, "it never happened. I fetched you as we arranged. We go on as we arranged. And Mr. Schultz is only a bad dream to which I owe ten pounds."

"And you're not angry? Then will you lend me some money to buy a hat, and then we will go straight on to London."

"Yes," said Edward, controlling Charles, who had just seen the peaches and thought they looked like something to eat. "But—if you won't think me a selfish brute I should like to say just one thing."

"Yes—" She wrinkled her brows apprehensively.

"Neither Charles nor I have had any luncheon. Would you very much mind if we—"

"Oh, how hateful of me not to remember!" she said. "Let me come and talk to you and feed Charles. What a darling he is! And you do forgive me, and you do understand? And we're friends again, just as we were before?"

"Yes. Just as we were."

"It's curious," she said, as they went back through the red and green and blue and yellow of the garden, "that I feel as though I knew you ever so much better, now we've quarreled."

Mr. Schultz had, it appeared, after all, paid for the two luncheons. Edward sent him two ten-pound notes and the sovereign, "with compliments and thanks."

"And that's the end of poor Mr. Schultz," she said, gaily, and, as it proved, with complete inaccuracy.

VIII

THE ROAD TO ———

THE drive to London was a silent one. Mr. Basingstoke did not want to talk; he had come on one of those spaces where the emotions sleep, exhausted. He felt nothing any more, neither anxiety as to the future nor pleasure at the nearness of the furry heap beside him under which, presently, his companion slumbered peacefully as a babe in its cot. His mind was blank, his heart was numbed; it was not till the car reached the houses spilled over the pretty fields like ugly toys emptied out of the play-box of a giant child, that mind or heart made any movement. Then it happened that the breeze caught the edge of the fur and lifted it, and he saw her little face softly flushed with sleep, lying very near him, and his heart seemed all at once to come to life again with an awakening stab of something that was not affection or even passion, but a kind of protective exultation—a deep, keen longing to take care of, to guard, to infold safely from all possible dangers and sorrows her who slept so happy-helpless beside him. Then his mind awoke, too, and he found himself wondering. The Schultz episode, his suspicions, resentment—the explication—all this should, one would have thought, have brushed, like a rough hand, the bloom from the adventure. And, instead of taking anything away, it had, even as she had said, added a soft touch of intimacy to their friendship. Further, he now in his heart had the memory that, for an instant, his thoughts had wronged her, that he had suspected her of wavering, almost of light-mindedness, though his thought had taken no such definite lines even to itself in its secret heart—and all the time there had only been thought for him, sincere, delicate consideration, and, in the matter of that man's accepted help, the trust of a child, and that innocence of Una before which even lions like Schultz become shy and safe. Imagine a subject who has suspected his princess of being, perhaps, not a princess at all, but one masquerading in the robes and crown of a princess . . . when he shall find her to be indeed royal, to what an ecstasy of loyalty will not his heart attain? So it was now with Mr. Basingstoke. He caught the corner of the fur and reverently covered the face of his princess.

THE INCREDIBLE HONEYMOON

And now the houses were thick and the shops began to score the streets with lines of color. He stopped at one of those big shops where they sell everything, and she awoke and said, "Are we there?"

"I thought," said he, "that you said something about a hat."

"Here?" she said, looking at the shop with strong distaste.

"Better here than really in London, I thought. And you'll want other things. And do you mind buying a box or a portmanteau or something? Because hotels like you to have luggage."

"I've been thinking—" she said, but he interrupted her.

"Forgive me," he said, "but even you cannot think your best thoughts when you're asleep."

Then she laughed. "Well, you must give me the money," she said, holding out a bare, unashamed hand, "because I haven't any."

He composed himself to wait, and he waited a long time, a very, very long time. He cheered the waiting by the thought that she could not, after all, have found the shop so unsuitable as it had, at the first glance, seemed. He watched the doorway, and his eye became weary of the useless snippets of lace and silk at something eleven-three with which the windows at each side of the door

THE ROAD TO ——

were plastered. He noticed the people who went in, and the many more who waited outside and longed for these absurd decorations—longed with that passion which, almost alone of the passions, a girl may display to the utmost immoderation without fear of censure or of shame. He observed the longing in the eyes of little, half-developed, half-grown girls for this or that bit of worthless frippery; he would have liked to call to them and say, "My dear children, do go in and buy yourself each a fairing, and let me pay." But he knew that so straightforward and simple a kindness would draw on him and on the children shame and censure almost immeasurable. So he just sat and was sorry for them, till he saw two of them titter together and look at him.

Then he got out of the car and went into the shop—they sold toys there as well as everything else—to buy something himself. He could not find exactly what he wanted—in shops crowded with glittering uselessnesses it is rarely that you can find the particular uselessness on which you have set your heart—but Tommy of the Five Bells had no fault to find with the big, brown-papered parcel which reached him by the next day's afternoon post. He could not imagine any soldiers more perfectly satisfying than these, no bricks more solid and square, no drafts more neatly turned, no dominoes more smoothly finished. To Mr. Basingstoke's old nurse the world seemed to hold nothing fairer than the lace collar and the violet-silk necktie. "Do me for Sundays for years," she said, putting them back in their tissue-paper and turning her attention to the box of sweets and the stockings for the children. The girl who sold Mr. Basingstoke the lace collar sniggered apart with a kindred sniggerer as she sold it to him, and delayed to make out his bill, but the other girl, almost a child, with a black bow tying her hair, sold him the stockings and was sympathetic and helpful.

"How many stockings ought a child to have, so as to have plenty?" he asked her, confidentially. At the lace-counter he had made his own choice, in stern silence.

"Three pairs," said the girl; "that's one in wear, one in the wash, and one in case of accidents." She glanced through the glass door at the motor, and decided that he could afford it. "But, of course, four would be better."

"I should think six would be best," said he, "that's one for each day in the week, and on Saturday they can stay in bed while their mother does the washing."

"You don't wash on Saturdays," said the girl, her little, plain face lighting up with a smile. She saw the eye of the shop-walker on her and added, nervously, "Shall we say six, then, sir; and what size? I mean what aged child? About what price?"

"Three to eleven," said he.

"They're one and eleven-three," said she.

"I mean the children, not the stockings—there are five of them—what's five sixes?"

"Thirty," the girl told him, with a glance at the shop-walker that was almost defiant in its triumph.

"That's it, then," said he, "and sort out the sizes properly, please, will you? Three six, two sevens, ten and eleven. And put in some garters—children's stockings are always coming down, you know—"

The girl had not before sold garters to insane but agreeable gentlemen. She hesitated and said in a low voice, "I don't think garters, sir. Suspenders are more worn now—"

"Well, suspenders then. The means doesn't matter—it's the keeping up that's the important thing." He laid a five-pound note on the counter, just as the shop-walker came up to her with a slightly insolent, "Serving, Miss Moore?"

"Sign, sir," said Miss Moore, defending herself from his displeasure with the bill. "Anything more, sir?"

"I want some sweets," said Edward, and was

THE INCREDIBLE HONEYMOON

directed to "the third shop on the left, through there."

It was not till two weeks later that a satined and beribboned box of sweets arrived by post for Miss Moore. "From Mary," said the legend within, and the postmark was Warwick. Mr. Basingstoke counted on every one's having at least one relation or friend bearing that commonest and most lovely of all names. And he was right. A distant cousin got the credit of the gift, which made the little apprentice happy for a day and interested for a week—exactly as Mr. Basingstoke had intended. His imagination pleased him with the picture of the sudden surprise of a gift, in that drab and subordinated life. By such simple means Mr. Basingstoke added enormously to his own agreeable sensations. And by such little exercises of memory as that which registered Miss Moore's name and the address of the shop he made those pleasures possible for himself. The sweets he bought on that first day of his elopement went to his nurse. He might have added more gifts, for the pleasure of spending money was still as new as nice, but the voice of Charles without drew him from the shop to settle a difference of opinion between that tethered dog and the chauffeur.

"Wanted to hang hisself over the side of the

car," the man explained, "and no loss to his mourning relations, if you ask me," he added, sourly.

Edward had hardly adjusted the situation before she came out—and he felt the sight of her was worth waiting for. She wore now a white coat with touches of black velvet, and the hat was white, too, with black and a pink rose or two.

"It looks more like Bond Street than Peckham," he said as she got in. "It surpasses my wildest dreams."

"I had to make them trim it," she said, "that's why I was such ages. All the ones they had were like Madge Wildfire—insane, wild, unrelated feathers and bows born in Bedlam."

Her eyes, under the brim of the new hat, thrilled him, and when Charles, leaping on her lap, knocked the hat crooked, scattered the mound of parcels, and made rosetted dust-marks on the new cloak, her reception of these clumsy advances would have endeared her to any one to whom she was not already dear.

"Well," she said, tucking Charles in between them, setting the hat straight, and dusting the coat, all in one competent movement, "have you had time yet to think what you're going to do with me?"

THE INCREDIBLE HONEYMOON

"I have had time," he said, rearranging the mound.

"I'm so sorry I was so long, but . . ."

"It was worth it," he said, looking at the hat. "Well, what I propose is that you should go, not to Claridge's, which is just the place where your relations will look for you, but to one of those large, comfortable hotels where strictly middle-class people stay when they come up to London on matters connected with their shops or their farms. I will give you as long as you like to unpack your new portmanteau and your parcels. Then I'll call for you and take you out to dinner."

"But I thought we were going on tramp," she objected.

"Dinner first, tramping afterward," he said, "a long while afterward. I don't propose to let you tramp in those worldly shoes." They were new and brown and soft to look at—as soft as other people's gloves, he thought.

"Don't dress for dinner," he said as they drew up in front of the Midlothian Hotel. "And, I say, I expect it would be safer to dine here; it's absolutely the last place where any of your people would look for you."

The dress in which she rejoined him later was a walking-dress of dark blue melting to a half transparency at neck and sleeves.

THE ROAD TO ——

"I bought it at that shop," she said. "It isn't bad, is it? They said it was a Paris model—and, anyhow, it fits."

He wanted to tell her that she looked adorable in it, and that she would look adorable not only in a Paris model, but in a Whitechapel one. But he didn't tell her this. Nor did he tell her much else. The dinner owed to her any brightness that it showed when shelved as a memory. She exerted herself to talk. And it was the talk of a lady to her dinner partner—light, gay, and sparkling, anything but intimate—hardly friendly, even; polite, pleasant, indifferent. He did not like it; he did not like, either, his own inability to carry on the duet in the key she had set, and at the same time he knew that he could not change the key. The surge of the world was round them again, even though it was only the world of the provincial haberdasher and the haberdasher's provincial wife. The smooth, swift passage of laden waiters across the thick carpets of the dining-room; the little tables gay with pink sweet-peas and rosy-hued lamps; the women in smart blouses, most of them sparkling beadily; the rare evening toilettes, worn in every case with an air of conscious importance, as of one to whom wearing evening dress was a rare and serious exception to the rule of life; the buzz of conversation curiously softer and lower in pitch than the talk at the Ritz and the Carlton—all made an atmosphere of opposition, an atmosphere in which all that appeared socially impossible—which, under the stars last night, had seemed natural, inevitable—the only thing to do. This world to which he had brought her had, at least, this in common with the world which dines at the Carlton and the Ritz, that it bristled with the negation of what last night had seemed the simplest solution in the world. But it had only seemed simple, as he now saw, because the solution had been arrived at out of the world. Here, beyond any doubt, was the antagonism to all that he and she had planned. This was the world where the worst scandal is the unusual—where it would be less socially blighting to steal another man's wife than to set off on a tramp with a princess to whom you were tied neither by marriage nor by kinship.

It was a lengthy silence in which he thought these things. She, in the silence, had been making little patterns with bread-crumbs till the waiter swept all away, made their table tidy, and brought the dessert. She looked up from the table-cloth just in time to see Edward smile grimly.

"What is it?" she asked, a little timidly.

"I was only thinking," he said, "what a two-penny halfpenny business we've made of life, with

THE ROAD TO ——

our electric light and our motors and our ugly houses and our civilization generally. A civilization replete with every modern inconvenience! In the good old days nobody would have minded a knight and a princess traveling through the world together, or even around the world, for that matter. Whereas now . . ."

She looked at him, gauging this thought. And he knew that he had said enough to make a stupid woman say, "I thought you would want to back out of it." What would she say? For a moment she said nothing. Then, sure of herself as of him, she smiled and said:

"We're going to teach Nobody to mind . . . its own business."

And then he said what he had come near to being afraid she would say.

"You don't want to back out of it, then?" he said, and she shook her head.

"No," she answered, slowly, and then, after a pause, again, "No."

"You are willing to go through the wood with your faithful knight, Princess? He will be a faithful knight."

"Yes," she said, "I know."

And then suddenly he perceived what before had not been plain to him—that the elopement that had seemed to offer so royal a road to all

THE INCREDIBLE HONEYMOON

that he really desired was not a road, but a barrier. That he was now in a position far less advantageous than that of a man who meets a girl all hedged around with the machinery of chaperonage, since, whereas the courtship may, where there is chaperonage, evade and escape it, where there is none the lover must himself supply its need—must, in fine, be lover and chaperon in one. Far from placing himself in a position where love-making would be easy, he had set himself where it was well-nigh impossible. He who courts a lady in her own home, surrounded by all the fences set up by custom and convention, can, at least, be sure that if his courtship be unwelcome it will be rejected. The lady need not listen unless she will. But when the princess rides through the wood with the knight whom she has chosen to be her champion she must needs listen if he chooses to speak. She can, of course, leave him and his championing, but what sort of championship is it which drives the princess back to the very dragon from which it rescued her? Edward saw, with dismal exactness, the intolerable impossibilities of the situation. They would go on—supposing her friends didn't interfere—as friends and comrades, brother and sister, she more and more friendly, he more and more tongue-tied, till at last every spark of the fire of the great adventure was trampled out by the flat foot of habit.

She might—and probably would, since men and women invariably misunderstand one another—believe his delicate reticences to be merely the indications of a waning interest, and construe knightly chivalry into mere indifference. If he made love to her—who could not get away from the lovemaking without destroying that which made it possible—he would be a presuming cad. If he didn't, what could she think but that he regretted his bargain? As he sat there opposite his princess, alone with her among the thickly thinning crowd, he wondered whether out of this any happiness could come to them.

When he had proposed the elopement he had meant marriage; the incurable temperamental generosity which had prompted him to offer her the help of the escape, on her own terms, now seemed to him the grossest folly. Yet how could he have held the pistol to her head, saying, "No marriage, no elopement."

Her voice broke his reverie. "I am very tired," she said. "I think I'll say good night. Do you mind?"

He almost fancied that her lip trembled a little, like a child's who is unhappy.

"Of course you're tired," he said, "and, I say,

you don't mind my not having talked for the last few minutes? I've been thinking of you—nothing else but you."

"Yes," said she, "it all looks very different here, as you say. Perhaps it will look more different even than this to-morrow. Shall we start on our tramp to-morrow—or shall I just go back and let's forget we ever tried to do something out of a book? I think you will tell me honestly tomorrow whether you think I had better go back."

"To-morrow," he said, looking into her eyes, "I will tell you everything you wish to hear. We'll spend to-morrow in telling each other things. Shall we? Good night, Princess. Sleep well, and dream of the open road."

"I shall probably," said the princess, "dream of my aunts."

IX

THE MEDWAY

"IF you had a map and I could put my finger on any place I chose, I should open my eyes the least bit in the world and put my finger on the Thames," she said at the breakfast-table, where she had for the first time sat opposite to him and poured his coffee, looking as demurely domestic as any haberdasher's wife of them all.

"The Thames?" he said. "I know a river worth two of that. . . ."

"A river that's worth two of the Thames must be the river of Paradise."

"So it is," he assured her, "and probably the Thames is infested by your relations. For a serious and secret conference such as we propose to ourselves there is no place like the Medway."

She had thought the Medway to be nothing but mud and barges, and said so.

"Ah, that's below Maidstone. Above— But you'll see. Wear a shady hat and bring that conspirator-looking cloak you wore last night—the fine weather can't possibly last forever. Twenty minutes for breakfast, half an hour for a complete river toilette, and we catch the ten-seventeen from Cannon Street, easily."

"I haven't a complete river toilette. And you? I thought you left all your possessions at the Five Bells—"

"I am not the homeless orphan you deem me," he said, accepting kidneys and bacon from a sleepy waiter. "I have a home, though a humble one, and, what's more, it's just around the corner—Montague Street, to be exact. Next door to the British Museum. So central, is it not? Some inward monitor whispered to me, 'She will want to go on the river,' and I laid out the complete boating-man's costume, down to white shoes with new laces."

"Did you really think I should think of the river? How clever of you."

"I am clever," he said, modestly, "and good. It is better to be good than clever. That is why I cannot conceal from you that I never thought of the river till you spoke about it. But I really have some flannels, little as you may think it, and we'll stop and get some boating-shoes for you, if you want them. Only you'll have to buy them with lightning speed and change them at Yalding."

THE MEDWAY

"Is that the name of the place? How lovely! If I had a title I should like it to be Lady Yalding—or the Duchess of Yalding. Her Grace the Duchess of Yalding will give you some more coffee, if you like."

"Why come down in the world? You were a princess last night."

"Princess of where?" she asked.

"We will give a morning to a proper definition of the boundaries of your territory one of these days. Meantime, are you aware that I don't even know the name by which the common world knows you?"

"I know you don't," she said, "and I'd much rather you didn't. If I'm to be a princess I'll be the Princess of Yalding, and if she has to have another name we'll choose a new one. I should like everything to be new for our new adventure."

They got the shoes and they caught the train, and, now the little gritty walk from Yalding station was over, they stood on the landing-stage of the Anchor, looking down on a sort of Sargasso Sea of small craft that stretched along below the edge of the Anchor garden.

"The canoe would be nice," she said.

"It would not be nice with Charles," he said, firmly. "Charles's first conscious act after we became each other's was to upset me out of a canoe,

THE INCREDIBLE HONEYMOON

to the heartless delight of three picnic parties, four pairs of sweethearts, two dons, and a personal friend."

"If Charles is to come *in* the boat," she said, "perhaps that fishing-punt . . ."

"Water within, water without," he said, spurning the water-logged punt. "This little sculling-boat will do. No—no outriggers for us, thank you," he said to the Anchor's gloomy boatman, who came toward them like a sort of fresh-water Neptune with a boat-hook for trident.

"He might, at least, have smiled," she said, as the sour-faced Neptune man turned toward the boat-house. "I hope he'll give us red cushions and a nice, 'arty sort of carpet."

"You get no carpets here," he assured her. "Lucky if we have so much as a strip of cocoa-nut matting. This is not the languid, luxurious Thames. On the Medway life is real, life is earnest. You mostly pull a hundred yards, anchor and fish; or if you do go farther from harbor you open your own locks, with your own crowbar. The best people are always a bit shabby. You and I, no doubt, are the cynosure of every eye. Yes, that 'll do; we'll put the basket in the stern, then the ginger-beer here. We'll put the cloak over it to keep it cool. All right, thank you. Crowbar in? Right. Throw in the painter. Right."

THE MEDWAY

Neptune pushed them with his trident and the boat swung out into midstream. A few strokes took them out of sight of the Anchor, its homely, flowered garden, its thatched house, its hornbeam arbor; they passed, too, the ugly, bare house that some utilitarian misdemeanant has built next to it, then nothing but depths of willow copse, green and gray, and the grassy curves of the towing-path where the loosestrife grows, and the willow herb, the yellow yarrow, and the delicate plumes of the meadow-sweet.

> "'Blond loosestrife and red meadow-sweet among,
>   We tracked the shy Thames shore.'"

he quoted.

"It's like a passport," she said—"or finding that you haven't lost your ticket, after all—when people have read the same things and remembered them. But don't you love the bit that begins about 'the tempestuous moon in early June,' and ends up with the 'uncrumpling fern and scent of hay new-mown'? I wonder why it is that when people quote poetry in books you feel that they're Laura-Matilda-ish, and when they do it really you quite like it. Do you write poetry?"

He looked at her guiltily. "Look out to the left," he said; "there's an absolutely perfect thatched barn, and four oast-houses—you know,

THE INCREDIBLE HONEYMOON

where they dry the hops, with little fires of oak chips. Have you ever been in an oast-house? We will some day—"

She was silent as the boat slipped past the old farm buildings, the old trees, the long perfection of the barn, and the deep red and green of the mossy oast-house wall going down sheer to the smooth, brown water, and hung at crevice and cranny with little ferns and little flowers—herb-robert and stonecrop. The reflection, till his oars shattered it, was as perfect as the building itself, and she drew a deep breath and turned to look back as the boat slid past.

"You were right," she said, "it is a darling little river. And you *do* write poetry, don't you?"

"Is this the confessional or the Medway?" he asked.

"I know you do," she said. "Of course you do—everybody does, as well as they can, I suppose; I can't, but I do," she added, encouragingly. "We will write poems for each other, on wet nights in the caravan, about Nature and Fate and Destiny, and things like that—won't we?"

The quiet river, wandering by wood and meadow, bordered by its fringe of blossoms and flowering grasses, the smooth backwaters where leaning trees touched hands across the glassy mirror, and water-lilies gleamed white and starry,

THE MEDWAY

the dappled shadows, the arch of blue sky, the gay sunshine, and the peace of the summer noon all wrought in one fine spell to banish from their thoughts all fear and dismay, all doubts and hesitations. Here they were, two human beings—young, healthy, happy—with all fair things before them and all sad things behind. It seemed to them both, at that moment, that they need ask nothing more of life than a long chain of days like this. They were silent, and each felt in the other's silence no embarrassment or weariness, but only a serene content. Even Charles, overcome by the spirit of the hour, was silent, slumbering on the matting between them, in heavy abandonment.

The perfection of their surroundings left them free to catch the delicate flavor of the wonderful adventure—a flavor which the dust and hurry of yesterday had disguised and distorted a little.

He looked at her and thought, "It is worth while—it is indeed worth while"—and knew that if only the princess were for his winning the moment of rashness which only yesterday he had almost regretted would be in its result the most fortunate moment of his life.

She looked at him, and a little fear lifted its head and stung her like a snake. What if he were to regret the adventure? What if he were to like her less and less—she put it to herself like that—while she grew to like him more and more? She looked at his eyes and his hands, and the way the hair grew on brow and nape, and it seemed to her that thus and not otherwise should a man's hair and eyes and hands be.

But they did not look at each other so that their eyes met till the boat rounded the corner to the wier-pool below Stoneham Lock. Then their eyes met, and they smiled, and she said:

"I am very glad to be here."

It seemed to her that she owed him the admission. He took it as she would have wished him to take it.

"I am glad you like my river," he said.

She was very much interested in the opening of the lock gates and deplored the necessity which kept her in the boat, hanging on to the edge of the lock with a boat-hook while he wielded the crowbar. The locks on the Medway are primitive in their construction and heavy to work. There are no winches or wheels or artful mechanical contrivances of weights and levers and cables. There are sluices, and from the sluice-gates posts rise, little iron-bound holes in them, holes in which the urgent nose of the crowbar exactly fits. The boatman leans indolently against the tarred, unshaped tree trunk whose ax-wrought end is

THE MEDWAY

the top of the lock gate; the tree trunk swings back above the close sweet-clover mat that edges the lock; the lock gates close — slow, leisurely, and dignified. Then the boatman stands on the narrow plank hung by chains to each lock gate, and with his crowbar chunks up the sluice, with a pleasant ringing sound of iron on iron, securing the raised sluice with a shining iron pin that hangs by a little chain of its own against the front of the lock gate, like an ornament for a gentleman's fob. If you get your hand under the pin and the sluice happens to sink, you hurt your hand.

Slowly the lock fills with gentle swirls of foam-white water, slowly the water rises, and the boat with it, the long gates unclose to let you out—slow, leisurely, dignified—and your boat sweeps out along the upper tide, smoothly gliding like a boat in a dream.

Thus the two passed through Stoneham Lock and the next and the next, and then came to the Round Lock, which is like a round pond whose water creeps in among the roots of grass and forget-me-not and spearmint and wild strawberry. And so at last to Oak Weir Lock, where the turtle-doves call from the willow wood on the island where the big trees are, and the wide, sunny meadows where the sheep browse all day till the shepherd calls them home in the evening—the shepherd with his dog at his heels and his iron crook, polished with long use and stately as a crozier in a bishop's hand.

They met no one—or almost no one. At East Peckham a single rustic looked at them over the middle arch of the seven-arched bridge built of fine, strong stone in the days of the Fourth Edward, and at Lady White Weir a tramp gave them good day and said it was a good bit yet to Maidstone. He spat in the water, not in insolence, but contemplatively, and Edward gave him a silver token of good will and a generous pinch of dark tobacco, with a friendly, "Here's for luck."

"You're a gentleman," the tramp retorted, grudgingly, and spat again, and slouched off along the green path. These two were all. Not another human face did they see for all the length of their little voyage.

All the long and lovely way it was just these two and the river and the fields and the flowers and the blue sky and youth and summer and the sun.

At Oak Weir they put the boat through the lock, and under the giant trees they unpacked the luncheon-basket they had brought from the Midlothian—how far away and how incredibly out of the picture such a place now seemed!—and sat among the twisted tree roots, and ate and drank

THE MEDWAY

and were merry like children on a holiday. It was late when they reached the weir, and by the time the necessity of the return journey urged itself upon them the shadows were growing longer and blacker till they stretched almost across the great meadow. The shepherd had taken the sheep away, passing the two with a nod reserved, but not in its essence unfriendly. Edward had smoked a good many cigarettes, and they had talked a good deal. It was as he had said at their first meeting, they were like two travelers who, meeting, hasten to spread, each before the other, the relics and spoils of many a long and lonely journey.

"I wish we could have stayed here," she said at last. "If we had only had the sense to fold our tents, like the Arabs, and bring them with us, I suppose we could have camped here."

"It isn't only tents," he said; "it's all the elegancies of the toilette—brushes and combs and slippers. You must return to the *Caravansary* that guards these treasures. The nine-fifty-five will do us. But we haven't much more than time. There's the boat to pay for and the basket to get to the station. Come, Princess, if we could stay here forever we would, but since we can't we won't stay another minute."

Once in the boat, and in the lock, she leaned back, holding the edge of the lock with the boat-

THE INCREDIBLE HONEYMOON

hook, and with the other hand detaining Charles. She looked back dreamily on the day which had been, and she did not pretend that it had not been, the happiest day in her life. To be with one who pleased—he certainly did please—and to whom one's every word and look was so obviously pleasing! It is idle to deny that she felt smoothed, stroked the right way, like a cat who is fortunate in its friends. And now all days were to be like this. The crowbar began its chinking—once, twice—then a jarring sound, and a low but quite distinct "Damn!"

She started out of her dream.

"I beg your pardon," he was saying, "but I've caught my finger, like a fool. I can't do anything. Can you come here?"

"Of course." She stepped out of the boat. The water in the lock had hardly begun to subside. She took the painter and, holding it, went to him, Charles following with cheerful bounds. The sluice had slipped a little and its iron pin held his finger firmly clipped against the tarred wood below.

She did not cry out nor tremble nor do any of the things a silly woman might have done. "Tell me what to do," was all she said.

He told her how to hold the crowbar, how to raise the sluice so that the finger might be re-

THE MEDWAY

leased. She did it all exactly and carefully. When the finger was released he wrapped his handkerchief around it.

"Does it hurt?" she said.

And he said, "Yes."

"You must put it in the water," she said. "You can't reach it here. Come into the boat."

He obeyed her. She came and sat by him in the stern—sat there quite silently. No "I'm so sorry!" or "Can't I do anything?" Her hand was on Charles's collar. His eyes were closed. His finger was badly crushed; the blood stained the water, and presently she saw it. She kept her eyes fixed on the spreading splash of red.

"You haven't fainted, have you?" she said at last. "It's getting very dark."

"No," he said, and opened his eyes. She raised hers, and both perceived one reason for the darkness—the boat had sunk nine feet or so. The dark, dripping walls of the lock towered above them. While he had fought his pain and she her sympathy the lock had been slowly emptying itself. They were at the bottom, or almost, and up those smooth walls there was no climbing out.

"Push the boat against the lower gate," he said; and as she obeyed he added, "I must try to climb up somehow. I'll pitch the crowbar up on shore first. Where is it?"

THE INCREDIBLE HONEYMOON

"I left it on the lock gate," she said. "Wasn't that right?"

"It doesn't matter," he told her; but even as he spoke the sluice, which the weight of the water had held in place after the pin had been removed, now, as the waters above and below it grew level with each other, fell into its place with a splash and an echoing boom, and with the shock the crowbar fell from its resting-place on the tarred ledge and disappeared in the water below.

"Lucky it didn't fall on us," he said, and laughed. "It's no use my climbing out now, Princess. I couldn't open the gate, anyhow. We're caught like two poor little rabbits in a trap—or three, if you count Charles—and here we must stay till some one comes along with a crowbar. I dare say there'll be a barge by and by. D'you mind very much?"

"Not a bit," she assured him, cheerfully. "It's all my fault, anyhow, and, besides, I enjoy it. Let me tie your hand up, and then you must smoke till rescue comes."

"Aren't you cold?" he asked, for indeed the air was chill in that watery inclosure.

"Not a bit. I have my cloak," she said, and snuggled into it. "But you'll be cold. Have half—it's a student's cloak, eight yards around."

He accepted the offer, and they sat with the

cloak wrapped around them both, with Charles snuggling under the lower folds of it.

"If you hear a footstep or a whistle or anything, shout," he said. "I do wish I hadn't let you in for this. I hate a fool."

"I don't mind a bit, except about your finger. The bone isn't broken, is it?"

"No," he said; "I've just made a fuss about nothing. I hate a fool, as I said before."

She thought of the wet patch on the tarred wood and the red patch in the water, and he felt her shiver.

"It's very decent of you," said she, "not to scold me about leaving the crowbar there."

"A good Medway boatman should never be separated from his crowbar," he said, monitorily.

"I know that now," she said. "I ought to have known before. I hate a fool, too."

X

OAK WEIR LOCK

"IF it weren't for your finger——" said she.

"My finger is the just reward of idiocy and doesn't deserve any kind thought from you."

"If it weren't for that, I should rather enjoy it," she said. "There's plenty to eat left in the basket. Shall I get it out and let's have supper before it's quite dark? I do really think it's fun. Don't you?"

"That's right," said he, with a show of bitterness, "make the best of it out of pity for the insane idiot who landed you in this fix. Be bright, be womanly, never let me guess that a cold, damp lock and a 'few bits of broken vittles' are not really better than a decent supper and a roof over your head. A fig for the elegancies of civilization and the comforts of home! Go on being tactful. I adore it."

"I meant what I said," she answered, with gentle insistence. "I do rather like it. I'll whine about my dinner and my looking-glass, if you like, but I'll get the supper first. Isn't it glorious to think that there's no one at home—where the comforts and the elegancies are—no one to be anxious about us because we're late, and scold us when we get home? Liberty," she ended, reflectively, "is a very beautiful thing. I suppose no one is likely to come along this way till the shepherd comes in the morning?"

"We'll hope for better luck," said he. "I say, you'll never trust me to take care of you again after this silly business—"

"I don't know," she said, deliberately, "that I ever asked you to take care of me. Did I? You were to help me—yes, and you have helped me—but I don't think I want to be taken care of, any more than another man would want it. I was in a difficulty and you helped me. If you were in a difficulty and I helped you, you wouldn't expect me to take care of you forever, would you?"

"I don't know," he said. "If you hadn't been extraordinarily sensible I should still be there with my hand in the thumbscrew."

"Did you think," she asked, sweetly, "that all women were inevitably silly?"

Charles raised his head and growled.

"There," said she, "you see, even Charles repudiates the idea."

THE INCREDIBLE HONEYMOON

If this was so, Charles instantly repudiated the idea with more growls and the added violence of barks. She muffled him in the cloak and listened. A footstep on the towing-path.

"Hullo!" she called, and Edward added, "Hi, you there!" and Charles, wriggling forcefully among the folds of the cloak, barked again.

"That ought to fetch them, whoever they are," said Edward, and stood up.

Even as he did so a voice said, urgently and quite close above them. "'Ush, can't yer!" and a head and shoulders leaning over the edge of the lock came as a dark silhouette against the clear dark blue of the starry sky. For it was now as dark as a July night is—and that, as we know, is never really dark at all. "'Ush!" repeated the voice. "Shut up, I tell yer!" and, surprisingly and unmistakably, it was to the two in the boat that he was speaking. "Make that dawg o' yours choke hisself—stow it, can't yer! Yer don't want to be lagged, do yer? Yer aren't got 'arf a chants once any one knows you're 'ere. Don't you know you're wanted? The police 'll be along some time in the night, and then you're done for."

"I think," said Edward, with extreme politeness, "that you are, perhaps, mistaking us for acquaintances, whereas we are strangers to you. But if you could be so kind as to open the gates

126

OAK WEIR LOCK

and lend us a crowbar to get through the other locks you would not be the loser."

"I know yer, right enough," said the man. "Yer ain't no strangers to me. It was me as 'ired yer the boat up at the Anchor. The boss 'e sent me out to look for yer. Only 'e doesn't know I know about your being wanted. Least said soonest mended 's what I allus say. Where's yer crow got to?"

"In the water," said Edward; "dropped off the lock gate."

"Clumsy!" said the man, giving the word its full vocative value. "Whereabouts?"

"Just over there," said Edward.

"Then yer tuck up yer shirt-sleeve and run yer 'and down and pass that there crow up to me. There ain't not above two foot o' water in 'er, if there's that."

To your Medway man the lock is as unalterably feminine as his ship to a sailor.

It was she who plunged her arm in the water, and, sure enough, there was the crowbar lying quietly and tamely beside them—"like a pet poodle," as she said.

"Give me ahold of that there crow," said the man. He lay face downward and reached down an arm. Edward stood on the thwart and reached up. The crowbar changed hands, and

THE INCREDIBLE HONEYMOON

the head and shoulders of the deliverer disappeared.

"I don't see what he wants the bar for," said Edward. "The lock's empty. Perhaps he means to go on ahead and open the other locks for us. I wonder who he took us for, and what the poor wretches are 'wanted' for—"

"It's a sinister word in that connection, isn't it?" said she. "Wanted!"

They pushed the boat toward the lower lock gate and held on to the lock-side, waiting till the lock gate should open and they should be able to pass out and begin their journey down the river to the Anchor. But the gates did not open, and almost at once a tremor agitated the boat. Edward tightened his grip of the boat-hook as the incoming rush of water took the boat's nose and held it hard.

"The idiot!" he said. "The silly idiot! He's filling the lock."

He was, and the rush of the incoming water quite drowned any remonstrances that might have been addressed to him. Boat and water rose swiftly, the upper gates opened, and, as they passed through, their deliverer laid his hand on the gunwale, as though to aid the boat's passage. But, instead, he stopped it.

"See 'ere, gov'ner," he said, low and hoarse

and exactly like a conspirator, "I couldn't bleat it out for all the country to hear while yer was down in the lock, but I knows as you're wanted and yer may think it lucky it's me as come after yer and not the gov'ner nor yet the police."

"I do really think," said she, softly, "that you're making a mistake. The police don't really want us."

"Oh, I got a bit of candle," was the unexpected rejoinder. "Get the young lady to hold the cloak up so as it don't shine from 'ere to Tunbridge to give yer away like, and yer light the dip and 'ave a squint at this 'ere."

He held out the candle and matches and a jagged rag of newspaper.

"'Ere," he said, "'longside where I'm 'olding of it."

She made a sort of screen of the cloak. Edward lit the candle, and when the flame had darkened and brightened again he read as follows:

MISSING—Young lady, height five feet six, slight build, dark hair and eyes, pale complexion. Last seen at Jevington, Sussex. Wearing black chiffon and satin dress, black satin slippers, and a very large French circular cloak with stitched collar. Has no money and no hat. Twenty pounds will be paid to any one giving information as to her whereabouts.

"Well," said Edward, blowing out the candle, "this lady has a hat, as you see, and she hasn't a black dress and satin slippers. Thank you for letting us through; here's something to get a drink with. Hand over the crowbar, please, and good night to you."

"Not so fast, sir," said the man, still holding on, "and don't make to jab me over the fingers with the boat-'ook, like what you was thinking of. I'm your friend, I am. I see that piece in the paper 'fore ever a one of them, but I never let on. That's why the gov'ner sent me, 'cause why—'e didn't think I knowed, and 'e means to 'ave that twenty pounds hisself."

"But," said she, "you see, I have got a hat and—"

"Yes, miss," said the man, "an' you've got the cloak, large and black and stitched collar, and all; it's that what's give yer away."

"But supposing I *was* the young lady," she said, grasping Edward's arm in the darkness, and signaling to him not to interfere with feminine diplomacy, "you wouldn't give me up to the police, would you? I wouldn't give you up if the police wanted you."

"'Course I wouldn't," he answered, earnestly. "Ain't that what I'm a-saying? I'm 'ere to 'elp yer do a bolt. The minute I saw that there bit in the paper I says to myself, 'It's them,' and why shouldn't I 'ave the twenty pounds as well as any one else?"

OAK WEIR LOCK

"There," said Edward, in a low voice, "you see! Let me deal with him."

But again her hand implored. "You're going to give us up to the police for twenty pounds?" she said, reproachfully.

He groaned. "'Ow yer do talk!" he said. "Women is all alike when it comes to talking. Stop talking and listen to me. Can't yer understand plain words? What yer got to do is to leave the boat at Mutton Worry Lock—that's three locks up—bunk across the fields to Tunbridge. If yer got money enough—and I'm sartain yer 'as, by the looks of yer—yer 'ire one of them motors and get away as fast as yer can. Get one at the Castle. Say yer going to Brighton, and when yer get away from the town tell the chap to drive t'other way."

"That's a good plan," said she.

"I mapped it all out as I come along," he said, with simple pride. "And, mind yer, I'm trusting yer like I shouldn't have thought I'd 'a' trusted nobody. 'Ave yer got the twenty pounds about yer?" he asked, anxiously.

"No," said she.

"Can't be helped, then." He breathed a sigh of resignation. "I'll just give yer my direction and yer send the ready to me. 'Oo says I don't trust yer?"

THE INCREDIBLE HONEYMOON

"You mean," said Edward, slowly, and would not be checked any longer by that hand on his arm—"you mean that you expect us to give you twenty pounds not to give us up to the police? The police have nothing to do with us. The whole thing's moonshine. Take your hand off the boat and get along home."

"Any man," said he who had been called Neptune—"any man as had the feelings of a man would think of this—young lady. Even if yer was to prove to Poad as yer wasn't wanted for nothin' criminal—it's none so easy to make Poad see anything, neither"—he ended, abruptly, and began anew. "Look 'ere, gov'ner, on account of your lady I say do a bolt. An' why should I be the loser? I only got to stick to the boat, whichever way yer go—up and down—and soon as yer land where there's a copper, lagged yer'll be to a dead cart, and only yourself to thank for it. Whereas I'm only trying to be your friend, if you'd only see it."

"I don't see why you should be so friendly," said Edward, now entirely losing control of the situation.

"Nor I shouldn't see it, neither, if it was only you," was the rejoinder.

"He's quite right," she whispered. "Promise what he wants and let's get away. I know exactly

OAK WEIR LOCK

what Poad is like. We should never make him understand anything. I couldn't bear it. Let's go. If you've got twenty pounds, give it to him and let's go."

"Think of your young lady," repeated the voice out of the darkness. "If yer promise to let me 'ear by the post, I'll take your word for it. I'm your true friend, and I knows a gentleman when I sees one."

"If you were a true friend," said Edward, "you wouldn't want paying for minding your own business."

"Aw, naw," he said, "'old 'ard, gov'ner. Ain't it a man's own business when there's twenty pounds to be made? Says I to myself, if it's worth some one's while to pay the money to catch 'er, it's well worth the gentleman's while to shell out and keep 'er, and . . ."

"Oh, hold your tongue!" said Edward. "Go on ahead and get the next lock ready. I'll give you the money. The lady wishes it."

"She's got her 'ead the right way on," said the friend in need. "Pull ahead, sir."

"But you can't, with your finger like that," she said. "I'll pull."

"Why not let me?" Neptune suggested. "We'd get there in 'alf the time," he added, with blighting candor.

THE INCREDIBLE HONEYMOON

So Neptune pulled the boat up to Mutton Worry Lock and the two crouched under the cloak. Charles, who might have been expected to be hostile to so strange a friend, received him with almost overwhelming condescension. At Mutton Worry Lock the deliverer said:

"Now 'ere yer deserts the ship, and 'ere I finds 'er and takes her back. And look 'ere, sir, I'm nobody's enemy but my own, so I am. And of course if I was to 'ave the twenty pounds it's my belief I'd drink myself under the daisies inside of a week. Let me 'ear by the post—William Beale, care of the Anchor Hotel—and send me ten bob a week till the money's gone. It 'll come easier to yer, paying it a little at a time like—and better for me in the long run. Yer ought to be a duke, yer ought. I never thought you'd 'a' ris' to the twenty. I'd 'a' been satisfied with five—and that 'll show yer whether I'm a true friend or not."

"I really think you are," she said, and laughed gently. "Good-by."

"Good evening, miss, and thank yer, I'm sure. Never say good-by; it's unlucky between friends."

"Here's a sovereign," said Edward, shortly. "Good night. You're jolly fond of the sound of your own voice, aren't you?"

"Sort of treat for me, sir," said Beale, always eagerly explanatory. "Don't often 'ear it. D'you know what they calls me at the Anchor, owing to me 'aving learnt to keep my tongue atween my teeth, except among friends? 'William the Silent's' my pet name. A gent as comes for the angling made that up, and it stuck, it did. Bear to the left till you come to the boat-'ouse, cater across the big meadow, and you'll hit Tunbridge all right, by the Printing Works. So long, sir; so long, miss."

Thus they parted.

"What an adventure!" she said; "and I believe William the Silent believes himself to be a model of chivalrous moderation. He would have been satisfied with five pounds."

"I believe he would, too," said Edward, with a grudging laugh. "It's your *beaux yeux*. The man has gone home feeling that he has as good as sacrificed fifteen pounds to a quixotic and romantic impulse. Wretched blackmailer though he is, he could not resist a princess."

"I like William," she said, decisively. "After all, as he says, one must live. Let's leave the cloak under this hedge. Shall we? It's like getting rid of the body. And I'll buy a flaxen wig to-morrow. And do you think it would be a help if I rouged a little and wore blue spectacles? It will be the saving of us, of course."

THE INCREDIBLE HONEYMOON

"I hope to heavens we get a motor in Tunbridge," said he. "You must be tired out."

"I'm not in the least tired," she said. "I'm stepping out like a man, don't you think? I've enjoyed everything beyond words. What a world it is for adventures once you step outside the charmed circle of your relations. Look at all the things that have happened to us already!"

"I didn't mean anything to happen except pleasant things," said he.

"Ah!" she said, with a fleeting seriousness, "life isn't like that. But there's been nothing but pleasant things so far—at least, almost nothing."

"Won't you take my arm?" he said.

"What for?"

"To help you along, I suppose," he said, lamely.

She stopped expressly to stamp her foot. "I don't want helping along," she said. "I'm not a cripple or a baby—and—"

He did not answer. And they walked on in silence through the starry, silent night. She spoke first.

"I don't want helping along," she said. "But I'd like to take your arm to show there's no ill-feeling. You take an arm on the way to dinner," she assured the stars, "and why not on the way to Tunbridge?"

The way to Tunbridge was short. They found

OAK WEIR LOCK

a car, and the night held no more adventures for them.

But in a sheltered nook in the weir stream below Jezebel's Lock a candle set up on a plate illuminated the green of alder and ash and the smooth blackness of the water, shedding on a lonely supper that air as of a festival which can only be conferred by candle-light shining on the green of growing leaves. There, out of sight of the towing-path, Mr. William Beale, charmed to fancy and anticipation by the possession of a golden milled token, made himself a feast of the "broken vittles" in the derelict Midlothian basket, and in what was left of the red wine of France toasted the lady of his adventure.

"'Ere's to 'er," he said to the silence and mysteries of wood and water. "'Ere's to 'er. She was a corker, for sure. Sight too good for a chap like 'im," he insisted, adding the natural tribute of chivalry to beauty; drank again and filled his pipe. Edward, from sheer force of habit, had smoothed the parting with tobacco.

"Not but," said William the Silent—"not but what I've known worse than 'im, by long chalks. Ten bob a week—and 'e'll send it along, too—good as a pension. 'E'll send it along."

He did. William the Silent had not misjudged his man.

XI

THE GUILDHALL

"WHERE is Charles?" she asked next day. Edward had called for her early, had paid the Midlothian's bill and tipped the Midlothian's servants, and now they were in a taxi on their way to Paddington. She had definitely put her finger on the map that morning, and its tip had covered the K's of Kenilworth and Warwick. She was still almost breathless with the hurry with which she had been swept away from the safe anchorage of the hotel, "and couldn't we have the hood down?" she added.

"Charles," said Edward, "is at present boarded out at a mews down Portland Road way, and I think we'd better keep the hood up. Look here! I never thought of the newspapers. This is worse than ever."

He handed her the *Telegraph*. Yesterday's advertisement was repeated in it—with this addition:

May be in company with tall, fair young man. Blue eyes, military appearance. Possesses large, white bull-terrier.

THE GUILDHALL

"Oh dear! They'll track us down," she said, and laughed. "What sleuth-hounds they are! But they can't do anything to me, can they? They can't take me back, I mean. I'm twenty-one, you know. Can't you do as you like when you're twenty-one?"

She looked at the paper again, and now her face suddenly became clouded and her eyes filled with tears. "I never thought of that." She hesitated a moment and handed him the paper, pointing to the place with the finger that had found Warwick and Kenilworth. Below the advertisement touching the young man and the bull-terrier, he read:

SILVER LOCKS—Come back. I am ill and very anxious.
AUNT ALICE.

"That means . . . ?"

"It means me. I'm Silver Locks—it's her pet name for me. I called my aunts the three bears once, when I was little, in fun, you know. And the others were angry—but *she* laughed and called me Silver Locks. And she's called it me ever since. I never thought about her worrying. What am I to do? I must go back. I thought it was too good to last, yesterday," she added, bitterly.

He put the admission away in a safe place, whence later he could take it out and caress it, and said, "Of course you must go back if you want

THE INCREDIBLE HONEYMOON

to. But don't do it without thinking. We meant to talk over our plans yesterday, but somehow we didn't. Let's do it to-day."

"But I can't go to Warwick. I must go back to her—I must."

"If you do," he said, "you won't go back to just her—you'll go back to the whole miserable muddle you've got away from. You'll go back to your other aunts and to your father. Besides, how do you know who put that advertisement in? Think carefully. Is the advertisement like her?"

"It's like her to be anxious and kind," said she.

"I mean, is she the sort of woman to advertise that she's ill? To advertise your pet name—and her own name—so that every one who knows you both and sees the advertisement will know that you are being advertised for? Is that like her?" He ended, astonished at his own penetration.

"No," she said, slowly, "it isn't. And it isn't like her to say she's ill. She never complains."

"She wouldn't use her illness as a lever to move events to her liking?"

"Never!" she said, almost indignantly.

"Then I think that this advertisement is some one else's. Where does she live."

"Hyde Park Square."

"Let us telegraph her, and not go to Warwick."

THE GUILDHALL

They stopped the taxi and composed a message. He despatched it.

Did you put advertisement in paper to-day? And are you ill? I am quite well and will write at once. Wire reply to Silver Locks, General Post-Office.

Then they told the man to drive around Regent's Park, to pass the time till there should be an answer.

In the park the trees were already brown, and on the pale, trampled grass long heaps of rags, like black grave-mounds, showed where weary men who had tramped London all night, moved on by Law and Order, inexorable in blue and silver, now at last had their sleep out, in broad sunshine, under the eyes of the richest city in the world. Little children, dirty and poor—their childhood triumphant over dirt and poverty—played happily in the grass that was less grass than dust.

"What a horrible place London is!" she said. "Think of yesterday."

That, too, he put away to be taken out and loved later.

"We won't stay in London," he said, "if the answer is what I think it will be. We'll go out into the green country and decide what we're going to do."

THE INCREDIBLE HONEYMOON

"But if she *did* put the advertisement in, it means that she's *very* ill. And then I must go to her."

"But if she didn't — and I more and more think she didn't—they may send some one to the General Post-Office post-haste—so it won't do for you to go for the telegram. Do you know the Guildhall Library?"

"No."

"It's a beautiful place—very quiet, very calm. And the officials are the best chaps I've ever found in any library anywhere. We'll go there. You must want to look up something. Let's see—the dates of the publication of Bacon's works. Write your name in the book—any name you like, so long as it isn't your own; then ask one of the officials to help you, and go and sit at one of the side tables—they're like side chapels in a cathedral—and stay there till I come. You'll be as safe and as secret as if you were in the Bastille. And I'll baffle pursuit and come to you as soon as I can."

"Yes," she said, meekly.

"And don't worry," he urged. "The more I think of it, the more certain I am that it was not the aunt you like who wrote that advertisement—"

He was right. The telegram with which, an

THE GUILDHALL

hour later, he presented himself at the Guildhall Library ran thus:

I did not write advertisement and I am not specially ill, but I am very anxious. Write at once. Aunt Loo and Aunt Enid are both here. I think they must have inserted the advertisement. A.

"Your Aunt Alice is a sportsman," he said, "to warn you like that."

"I told you she was a darling," she answered—and her whole face had lighted up with relief—"and you are the cleverest person in the world! I should never have thought about its not being her doing, never in a thousand years. You deserve a medal and a statue and a pension."

"I don't deserve more than I've got," said he, "nor half so much. The sun shines again."

She flashed a brilliant smile at him, and pushed a brown book along the table.

"I suppose we ought to look studious," she said, "or they'll turn us out. I am so glad Aunt Alice isn't really worse. You don't know how I've felt while you've been away. It seemed so horribly selfish—to have been so happy and all while she was ill and worried. But, of course, you do know."

"Let us go out," he said, putting the books together.

"Yes," she said, "I know all about Bacon. Not that I'll ever want to know."

"I'm not so sure," said he. "Did it ever occur to you that perhaps the Baconians are right, and he was an intellectual giant, almost like Plato and Aristotle rolled into one? We'll go to Stratford some day, and look at Shakespeare's bust and see if we think he could have written 'The Tempest.'"

"You shouldn't judge people by their faces," she said. "Handsome is as handsome does."

"Oh, but you should," said he. "It's handsome does as handsome is. I always go by appearances. Don't you? But of course, I know you do—"

She opened one of the books and began to turn the pages. "Look what I found," she said, and all the time their voices had been lowered to the key of that studious place. "Look, isn't it pretty? And do you see?—the e's are like the Greek θ. Can you read it?"

He read:

> "Fair Lucrece, kind Catherine, gentle Jane,
> But Maria is the dearest name.
>   Robert Swinford, 1863."

"Yes, that's what I make it. It doesn't rhyme, but I expect Maria was very pleased. Do you think they were studying with a stern tutor, and he wrote that and pushed it over to her when no

THE GUILDHALL

one was looking? It's an odd thing to have written in a Natural History book. There's something more on another page—but it doesn't make sense:

"I am true rew Hebrew—CXIX—101."

"I expect he was just trying a pen. Come, the librarian has his scholarly eye on you."

"I should like to look through all the old books and find out all the names people have written and make stories about them," she said, and he received the curious impression that she was talking against time; there was about her a sort of hanging back from the needful movement of departure. He picked the books up and carried them to the counter, she following, and they walked in silence down the gallery hung with Wouvermans and his everlasting gray horse.

"Let's go into the Hall," he said. So they turned under the arch and went into the beautiful great vaulted Guildhall, where the giants Gog and Magog occupy the gallery, and little human people can sit below on stone benches against the wall, and gaze on the monuments of the elder and the younger Pitt, and talk at long leisure, undisturbed and undisturbing, which is not the case in the Library, as Edward pointed out.

"Now, then," he began.

THE INCREDIBLE HONEYMOON

"Yes," she said, hurriedly. "Something will have to be done about Aunt Alice."

"Yes. But what?"

"I don't know." She turned and leaned one hand on the stone seat so that she faced him. "You do believe that I don't regret coming away? I think it would have been splendid to have gone on—like yesterday—but you see it's impossible."

"No, I don't," he said, stoutly.

She made a movement of impatience. "Oh yes, it is—quite," she said. "However rich you are, you can't go on forever being blackmailed. Every one would know us, or else you'd have to give up Charles, and even then I expect you'd be obliged to pay twenty pounds every three-quarters of an hour. It can't be done. And, besides, we should never know a moment's peace. Wherever we went we should imagine a blackmailer behind every bush, and every one we spoke to might be a detective. It's no use. I must go back. Do say you know I must."

"I don't."

"Well, say you know I don't want to."

"I can't say that . . . because, if you don't want to . . . there's always the old alternative, you know." He was looking straight before him at the majestic form of the Earl of Chatham.

"What alternative?"

THE GUILDHALL

"Marrying me," he said, humbly. "Do. I don't believe that you'd regret it."

"When I marry," she said, strongly, "it won't be just because I want to get myself out of a scrape."

"I hoped there might be other considerations," he said, still gazing at the marble. "You were happy yesterday. You said so."

"You talk as though marrying were just nothing—like choosing a partner for a dance. It's like—like choosing what patterns you'd be tattooed with, if you were a savage. It's for life."

"And you can't like me well enough to choose me?"

"I do like you," she answered, with swift and most disheartening eagerness, "I do like you awfully; better than any man I've ever known— oh, miles better—not that that's saying much. But I don't know you well enough to marry you."

"You don't think it would turn out well?"

She faltered a little. "It—it mightn't."

"We could go on being friends just as we are now," he urged.

"It wouldn't be the same," she said, "because there'd be no way out. If we found we didn't like each other, to-morrow, or next month, or on Tuesday week, we could just say good-by and

THE INCREDIBLE HONEYMOON

there'd be no harm done. But if we were married—no—no—no!"

"Do you feel as though you would dislike me by Tuesday week?"

"You know I don't," she said, impatiently, "but I might. Or you might. One never knows. It isn't safe. It isn't wise. I may be silly, but I'm not silly enough to marry for any reason but one."

"And that?"

"That I couldn't bear to part with him, I suppose."

"And you can bear to part with me. There hasn't been much, has there? Just these three days, and all our talks, and . . ." He stopped. A tear had fallen on her lap. "I won't worry any more," he said, in an altered voice. "You shall do just what you like. Shall I get a taxi and take you straight to your aunt's? I will if you like. Come."

"There's no such hurry as all that," she said, "and it's no use being angry with me because I won't jump over a wall without knowing what's on the other side. No, why I should jump, either," she added, on the impulse of a sudden thought. "You haven't told me that yet. What good would my getting married do to Aunt Alice? I don't mean that I would, because you know I couldn't

THE GUILDHALL

—even for her—but what good would it do if I did?"

"If we were married," he said, with a careful absence of emotion, "we could send your aunt a copy of our marriage certificate and a reference to my solicitor. She would then know that you had married a respectable person with an assured income, instead of which you now appear to be running about the country stealing ducks with Heaven knows who."

"Yes," she said, "I see that. Oh, I have a glorious idea! It will suit you and me and Aunt Alice and make everybody happy!—like in books. Let's have a mock marriage, and forge the certificate."

"Have you ever seen a marriage certificate?"

"No, of course not."

"Well, it would be as difficult to forge as a bank-note."

"Why—have you ever seen one?" she asked, and he hoped it was anxiety he read in her tone.

"Yes; I know a chap who's a registrar. I've witnessed a marriage before now."

"Then there's no need to forge," she said, light-heartedly. "Your friend would give you one of the certificates, of course, if you asked him, and we could fill it in and make Aunt Alice happy."

He laughed, and the sound, echoing in the gray

emptiness of the Hall, drew on him the sour glance of a barrister, wigged and gowned, hastening to the mayor's court.

"He's wondering what you've got to laugh at," she said, "and I don't wonder. *I* don't know. Why shouldn't we pretend to be married? I'm sure your friend would help us to. Oh, do!" she said, clasping her hands with an exaggerated gesture that could not quite hide the genuine appeal behind it. "Then we sha'n't have to part. I mean I sha'n't have to go back to the aunts and all the worry that I thought I'd got away from."

"You're not really serious."

"But I am. You will—oh, do say you will."

"No," he said, "it's impossible—Princess, don't ask if I can't."

"Then it's all over?"

"I suppose so, if you insist on going back."

"I don't insist. But I must do something about Aunt Alice. She's always been a darling to me. I can't go away and be happy and not care whether she's miserable or not. You'd hate me if I could. I'll go back to-morrow or to-night. You said we should go into the country and think things out. At least we can do that—we can have one more day. Shall we?"

Her sweet eyes tempted and implored.

"What sort of day would it be," he said, "with

THE GUILDHALL

the end of everything at the end of it? How could we be happy as we were yesterday?—for you were happy, you owned it. How could we be happy together when we knew we'd got to part in six hours—five hours—two hours—half an hour? Besides, why should I give you the chance to grow any dearer? So as to make it hurt more when you took yourself away from me? No—"

"I didn't know I was dear," she said, in a very small voice.

Perhaps he did not hear it, for he went on: "If the splendid adventure is to end like this, let it end here—now. I've had the two days; you can't take those from me."

"I don't want to take anything from you, but—"

"Let's make an end of it, then," he said, ruthlessly, "since that's what you choose. Good-by, Princess. Let's shake hands and part friends." He rose. "Let's part friends," he repeated, and paused, remembering that you cannot go away and leave a lady planted in the Guildhall. Yet he could not say, "Let us part friends, and now I will call a cab."

She was more expert. "At least," she put it, "we needn't part here in the dark among the images of dead people. Come out into the sunshine and look at the pretty pigeons."

He was grateful to her. In the Guildhall yard the cab would happen, if it happened at all, naturally and without any effect of bathos.

They stood watching the sleek birds strutting on little red feet, and fluttering gray wings in the sunshine. She thought of the wood-pigeon in the wood by the river, and the calm brightness of yesterday held out beckoning hands to her.

"I didn't think it was going to end like this," she said.

"Nor I," he answered, inexorably.

"Are you quite sure it's impossible? The mock marriage, I mean? In books it's always so frightfully easy, even when the girl isn't helping?"

"I'm afraid it's impossible," said he. "I wish it wasn't. Look at that blue chap," he added, indicating a fat pigeon for the benefit of a passing boy. "You must go back to your aunts. And I must go back to . . . oh, well, there's nothing much for me to go back to."

They were walking along King Street now. "It does seem rather as though a sponge were going to pass over the slate . . . and there wouldn't be much left," she said.

He glanced at her, suddenly alert. If she felt that . . . why, then . . .

He wished that the scene had not been in one of the most frequented streets of the City of Lon-

THE GUILDHALL

don. If it had been in a drawing-room, for instance—her drawing-room—it would have been possible to say the words of parting with something of dignity and finality. But here, with—in the background and not to be evaded—that snorting taxicab over whose closed door their farewells must be made. . . . But need it be across a taxicab door?

"Let us," he said, "take a cab. I will go with you as far as Hyde Park Square."

"Shall we have the hood down?" she asked, with intention. "It doesn't matter now if any one does see us." But he pretended not to hear, and the hood remained as it was.

They were silent all the crowded way along Cheapside, where there were blocks, as usual, and the drivers of lorries and wagons were cheerfully profane. Silent, too, along Newgate Street and New Oxford Street. The driver, being a wise man, turned up Bloomsbury Street to escape from the blocks in Oxford Street; they passed the British Museum and, presently, the Midlothian Hotel. And as they passed it, each thought of the breakfast there only that morning, when she had poured the coffee of one from whom she had then had no mind to part.

"Oh, why are we doing it?" She spoke suddenly, and her speech had the effect of a cry. "We didn't mean to say good-by, and now we're going to. Don't let's."

"But your aunt," he said, feeling as foolish as any young man need wish. "If you don't go back to her now you'll want to to-morrow—and I can't . . . I told you why I want to part now, if we are to part. Now, before it gets any worse."

"We shall be at Hyde Park Square in a minute," she said, desperately.

"Yes," he said, "it's nearly over. What number is it? I must tell the man."

"Tell him to turn around and go somewhere else—into the country; we said we would, you know. I'm not going back to Hyde Park Square. Tell him . . ."

"Princess," he said, "I can't bear it. Let him go on."

"But I'm not asking you to bear anything. Don't you understand?"

"Not . . .?"

"Yes, I will; if you'll ask me."

"You'll marry me?"

"Yes," she said, "rather than have everything end in absolute silliness, like this."

He looked at her, at her clasped hands and the frown of her great resolve. He perceived that he was worth something to her—that she was prepared to pay a price—the price he set—rather than

THE GUILDHALL

lose him altogether. Her eyes met his with a mingling of courage and desperation, as of one who has chosen a difficult and dangerous path, one who makes a great sacrifice, leads a forlorn hope. And his eyes dwelt for a moment on hers, appreciatively, thoughtfully. And in that moment his resolve was taken.

"No," he said, "you didn't want to jump the wall without knowing what it would be like on the other side. I won't have an unwilling wife. On the other hand, I won't lose you now, Princess, for a thousand fathers and ten thousand aunts. Make up your mind to the mock marriage, and that shall be the way out."

"But I thought you said it was impossible."

"So it was. But it isn't now. I've been thinking."

She leaned back, turned toward him from the corner, and faced him with fearless eyes.

"What a nightmare of a day it's been," she said. "Aren't you glad we're awake again? When can I send the certificate?" she asked, eager and alert.

"At the earliest possible moment," said he. "I must see my friend about it at once. Would you mind waiting for me—say in St. Paul's? And then we'll end our day in the country, after all."

"You are good," she said, and laid her hand for

a fleeting instant on his arm. "I do think it's good of you to give way about the mock marriage. You know I had really set my heart on it. Now everything will be plain sailing, won't it? And we'll go to Warwick the minute we're mock-married, because my putting my finger on it and Kenilworth ought to count, oughtn't it?"

"It shall," he said, gravely.

XII

WESTMINSTER

A WEDDING-DAY—even a real wedding-day—leaves at best but a vague and incoherent memory. To the bridegroom it is a confused whirling recollection of white satin and tears and smiles and flowers and music—or perhaps a dingy room with a long table and an uninterested registrar at the end of it.

Edward Basingstoke thought with regret of the flowers and the white satin. If he had accepted her submission, had consented to the real marriage, there should have been white roses by the hundred, and the softest lace and silk to set off her beauty. As it was—

"We shall have to go through some sort of form," he told her, "because of the clerks. If my friend were just to tear out a certificate and give it to us the people in the office . . . You understand."

"Quite," she said.

THE INCREDIBLE HONEYMOON

"It 'll be rather like a very dingy pretense at a marriage. You won't mind that?"

"Of course not. Why should I?"

"Then, if you're sure you really want to go through with it . . . shall we go to my friend's now, and get it over?"

"He doesn't mind?"

"Not a bit."

"He must be a very accommodating friend."

"He is," said Edward.

"Where did you leave the luggage?" she asked, suddenly. They were walking along the Embankment.

"At Charing Cross."

"Well, I'm going to get it. And I shall go to the Charing Cross Hotel with it, and you can meet me in three hours."

"But that 'll only just give us time," he said. "Why not come with me now?"

"Because," she said, firmly, "I won't play at mock marriages unless I like, and I won't play at all unless you let me do as I like first."

"Won't you tell me why?"

"I'll tell you when I meet you again."

"Where?" he asked. And she stopped at the statue of Forster in the Embankment Gardens, and answered:

"Here."

WESTMINSTER

Then she smiled at him so kindly that he asked no more questions, but just said:

"In three hours, then," and they walked on together to Charing Cross.

And after three hours, in which he had time to be at least six different Edwards, he met, by the statue of the estimable Mr. Forster, a lady all in fine white linen, wearing a white hat with a wreath of white roses around it, and long white gloves, and little white shoes. And she had a white lace scarf and a live white rose at her waist.

"I thought I'd better dress the part," she said, a little nervously, "for the sake of the clerks, you know."

"How beautiful you are," he said, becoming yet another kind of Edward at the sight of her, and looking at her as she stood in the afternoon sunshine. "Why didn't you tell me before how beautiful you were?"

"I . . . How silly you are," was all she found to say.

"I wish, though," he said, as they walked together along the gravel of the garden, "that you'd done it for me, and not for those clerks, confound them!"

"I didn't really do it for them," she said. "Oh no — and not for you, either. I did it for myself. I couldn't even pretend to be married in anything but white. It would be so unlucky."

All that he remembered well. And what came afterward—the dingy house with the grimy doorstep, and the area where dust and torn paper lay, the bare room, the few words that were a mockery of what a marriage service should be, the policeman who met them as they went in, the charwoman who followed them as they went out, the man at the end of the long, leather-covered table—Edward's old acquaintance, but that seemed negligible—who wished them joy with, as it were, his tongue in his cheek. And there was signing of names and dabbing of them with a little oblong of pink blotting-paper crisscrossed with the ghosts of the names of other brides and bridegrooms— real ones, these—and then they were walking down the sordid street, she rather pale and looking straight before her, and in her white-gloved hand the prize of the expedition, the marriage certificate, to gain which the mock marriage had been undertaken.

And suddenly the romantic exaltation of the day yielded to deepest depression, and Edward Basingstoke, earnestly and from the heart, wished the day's work undone. It was all very well to talk about mock marriages, but he knew well enough that his honor was as deeply engaged as though he had been well and truly married in Westminster Abbey by His Grace of York assisted by His Grace of Canterbury. Freedom was over, independence was over, and all his life lay at the mercy of a girl—the girl who, a week ago, had no existence for him. The whole adventure, from his first sight of her among dewy grass and trees, had been like a fairy-tale, like a romance of old chivalry. He had played his part handsomely, but with the underlying consciousness that it was a part—a part sympathetic to his inclinations, but a part, none the less. The whole thing had been veiled in the mists of poetry, illuminated by the glow of adventure. And now it seemed as though he had thoughtlessly plucked the flower of romance which, with patience and careful tending, would have turned to the fruit of happiness. He had plucked the flower, and all he had gained was the power to keep a beautiful stranger with him—on false pretenses. He wished that she, at least, had not so gaily entered on the path of deception. Never a scruple had disturbed her—the idea of deceiving an aunt who loved her had been less to her than—than what? Less, at least, than the pain of losing him forever, he reminded himself. He tried to be just—to be generous. But at the back of his mind, and not so very far back, either, Iago's words echoed, "She did deceive her father, and may thee." His part of the deception now seemed to him the blackest deed of his life, and he could not undo it. It was impossible to turn to this white shape, moving so quietly beside him, with:

"Let's burn the certificate. Deceit is dishonorable."

If she did not think so . . . well, women's code of honor was different from men's. And she *had* been willing to marry him in earnest, with no deceptions or reservations. This mock business had been, in the end, his doing, not hers. And now they had gone through with it, and here he was walking beside her, silent, like a resentful accomplice. They had walked the street's length, its whole dingy length, in silence. The light of life had, once more, for Mr. Basingstoke, absolutely gone out. They turned the corner, and still he could find nothing to say; nor, it appeared, could she. The hand with the paper hung loosely. The other hand was busy at her belt—and now the white rose fell on the dusty pavement, between a banana-skin and a bit of torn printed paper. He stooped, automatically, to pick up the rose.

"Don't," she said. "It's faded."

It so manifestly wasn't that he looked at her, and on the instant the light of life began to be again visible to him, very faint and far, like the

WESTMINSTER

pin-point of daylight at the end of a long tunnel, but still visible. For he now perceived that for her, too, the light had gone out—blown out, most likely, by the same breath of remorse. Sublime egoist! He was to have the monopoly of fine sentiments and regretful indecisions, was he? Not a thought for her, and what she must have been feeling. But perhaps what she had felt had not been that at all; yet something she had felt, something not happy—something that led to the throwing away of white roses.

"I can't let it lie there," he said, holding it in his hand. "I should like to think," he added, madly trying to find some words to break the spell that, he now felt, held them both—"I should like to think it would never fade."

She smiled at that—a small and pitiful smile.

"Cheer up," she said; "lots of people have got *really* married and then parted, as they say, at the church door. This is a perfect spot for a parting," she added, a little wildly, waving toward a corn-chandler's and a tobacconist's; "or, if your chivalry won't let you desert me in this desolate neighborhood . . . let me tell you something, something to remember; you'll find it wonderfully soothing and helpful. From this moment henceforth, forever, every place in the world where we are will be the best place for parting—if we want to part. Isn't that almost as good as the freedom you're crying your eyes out for?"

"I'm not," he said, absurdly; but she went on.

"Do you think I don't understand? Do you think I don't know how you feel twenty times more bound to me than if we were really married? Perhaps it's only because everything's so new and nasty. Perhaps you won't feel like that when you get used to things. But if you do—if you don't get over it then—it's all been for nothing, and we might as well have parted among the pigeons."

She walked faster and faster.

"What we have to remember—oh yes, it's for me as well as you—what we've got to remember is that we're to be perfectly free. We needn't stay with each other an instant after we wish not to stay. Doesn't that help?"

"You're a witch," he said, keeping pace with her quickened steps, "but you don't know everything. And you're tired and—"

"I know quite enough," she said.

Never had he felt more helpless. Their aimless walking was leading them into narrower and poorer streets where her bridal whiteness caught the eye and turned the head of every passer-by. The pavements were choked with slow passengers and playing children, small, dirty, pale, with the anxious expression of little old men and women.

WESTMINSTER

"Do you like deer?" he asked, suddenly.

"Deer?"

"Yes—fawns, does, stags, antlers?"

"Of course I do."

"Then let's go to Richmond Park. Let's get out of this."

The points of her white shoes showed like stars among the filth of the pavement, her clean, clear beauty shining against the drab and dirty houses like a lily against a dust-heap. He felt a surge of impotent fury that such a background should be possible. The children, tired and pale with the summer heat that had been so glad and gay and shining to him and to her yesterday on the quiet river, looked like some sort of living fungus—and their clothes looked like decaying vegetables. If Mr. Basingstoke had been alone he would have solaced himself by going to the nearest baker's and buying buns for every child in sight. But somehow it is very difficult to do that sort of thing unless you are alone or have a companion who trusts you and whom you trust beyond the limit of life's cheaper confidences. He felt that self-exculpatory eagerness to give which certain natures experience in the presence of sufferings which they do not share. Also he felt—and hated himself for feeling—a fear lest, if he should act naturally, she might think he wanted to "show

THE INCREDIBLE HONEYMOON

off." To show off what, in the name of all that was pretentious and insincere? Had civilization come to this, that a man was "showing off" who took want as he found it and changed it, without its costing him the least little loss or self-denial, into a radiant, if momentary, satisfaction? And yet, somehow, he found he could not say, "Let's go and raid the bun-shop for these kiddies."

"We're to pass our lives together, and I can't say a simple thing like that," he thought, with curious bitterness—but, indeed, all his thoughts were confused and bitter just then.

What a travesty of a wedding-day! He would have liked his wedding-feast to be in the big barn of the bride's father, and every neighbor, rich and poor, to have drunk their health in home-brewed ale of the best, and the tables cleared away and a jolly dance to follow, and when the fun was at its merriest he and she would have slipped out and ridden home to his own house on the white horse—Dobbin, his name—she on the pillion behind him, her arm soft about his waist, and the good horse so sure of foot that he never stumbled, however often his master turned his face back to the dear face over his shoulder. Instead of which she had consented to a mock marriage in a registry-office—and this.

WESTMINSTER

"Let's get out of this," he repeated.

"We are getting out of it," she said, and, abruptly, "Don't people who have real weddings pay the ringers and the beadle and give a feast to the villagers—open house, and all that?"

He thrilled to the magic of that apt capping of his thought.

"Yes," he said, and, not knowing why, hung on her next words.

"Couldn't we?" she said, and her eyes wandered to the rose he still carried. "Of course it was only pretending, but we might pretend a little longer. Couldn't we give our wedding-feast here? The guests are all ready," she added, and her voice trembled a little.

How seldom can man follow his desire. Edward would have liked to fall on his knees among the cabbage-stalks and the drifting dust and straw and paper—to kneel before her and kiss her feet. For, in that moment, and for the first time, he worshiped her.

The imbecile irrationality of this will not have escaped you. He worshiped her for the very thought, the very impulse of simple loving-kindness which he had been ashamed to let her know as his own.

She kindled to the lighting of his face. "I knew you would," she said. "You are a dear." The same irrational admiration shone in her eyes. "Sweets? Pounds and pounds of?"

"Buns," he answered, "buns and rock-cakes. Sweets afterward, if you like," and enthusiastically led the way to the nearest baker's.

Now this is difficult to believe and quite impossible to explain, but it is true. No human ear but their own had heard this interchange. "Sweets," "buns," and "rock-cakes," those words of power had, in fact, been spoken in the softest whisper, but from the moment of their being spoken a sort of wireless telegraphy ran down that mean street from end to end, and by the time they reached the baker's they had a ragged following of some fifty children, while from court and alley and narrow side-street came ever more and more children, ragged children, stuffily dressed children, children carrying bags, children carrying parcels, children carrying babies and jugs and jars and bundles. The crowd of children pressed around the baker's door, and noses flattened like the suckers of the octopus in aquariums marked a long line across the window a little above the level of the bun-trays. I do not pretend to explain how this happened. Good news proverbially travels fast. It also travels by ways past finding out.

She began to take the buns by twos and threes

from the tray in the window, and held them out. A forest of lean arms reached up and a shrill chorus of, "Me, teacher! Me!" varied by, "She's 'ad one—me next, teacher! Let the little boy 'ave one, lady; 'e 'ain't 'ad nuffin."

The woman of the shop rolled forward. She was as perfectly spherical as is possible to the human form.

"Treat, sir?" she said, in a thick, rich, husky voice (like cake, as Edward said later). They owned her guess correct.

"How much 'll you go to?"

"A bun apiece," said Edward.

"For the whole street? Why, there's hundreds!"

"The more the merrier," said Mr. Basingstoke.

"Do 'e mean it?" the woman asked, turning to the bun-giver.

"Yes, oh yes." The girl turned from the door to lean over the smooth deal counter. "It's our wedding-day," she whispered, "and we didn't give any wedding-breakfast, so we thought we'd give one now."

Edward had turned to the door and was making a speech.

"You shall all have a bun," he said, "to eat the lady's health in. But it's one at a time. Now you just hold on a minute and don't be impatient."

"Bless your good 'art, my dear," the globular

lady was wheezing into the ear of the mock bride. "Married to-day, was you? I'm sure you look it, both of you—every inch you do. But we 'aven't got the stuff in the place for 'arf that lot."

"How soon could you get it?"

"I could send a couple of the men out. Do it in ten minutes—or less, if Prickets around the corner's not sold out."

"How much will it cost—something for each of them—cake if not buns—sweets if not cake—?"

The round woman made a swift mental calculation and announced the result.

She who looked so much like a bride turned to him who seemed her bridegroom. "Give me some money, please, will you?"

Money changed hands, and changed again.

"Now, lookee 'ere," said the round one, "you let me manage this 'ere for you. If you don't you'll be giving three times over to the pushing ones, and the quiet ones won't get nothing but kicked shins and elbows in the pit of stomachs. I know every man jack of them 'cept the hinfans in arms, and even them I knows the ones as is carrying of them. Wait till I send the chaps off for the rest of the stuff."

The crowd outside surged excitedly, and the frail arms still waved to the tune of, "Me next, teacher!" All along the street the faces of the houses changed features as slatternly women and shirt-sleeved men leaned out of the windows to watch and wonder. When the baker's wife rolled back into the shop she found the girl silent, with lips that trembled.

"There, don't you upset yourself, my pretty," said the round one. "You'll like to give it to 'em with your own hands, I lay. Take and begin on what's before you—let 'em come in one door and out of the other, and I'll see as they don't come twice."

"You do it," said the girl, and she spoke to Edward over her shoulder. "I didn't think it would be like this. Tell them we've got to go, but Mrs. Peacock will give them each a bun."

"How clever of her to have noticed the name," he thought; but he said, "Are you sure you don't want to have the pleasure of seeing their pleasure?"

"No—no," she said. "Let's get away. I can't bear it. Mrs. Peacock will see to it for us—won't you?"

"That I will, lovey, and keep the change for you against you call again. You can trust me."

"We don't want any change," she said. "Spend it all on buns, or cake, or anything you like. It *is* good of you. Oh, good-by, and thank you—so much. I didn't think it would be like this," she said, and gave Mrs. Peacock both hands, while Edward explained to the crowd outside.

A wail of disappointment went up, but stayed itself as Mrs. Peacock rushed to the door.

"It's all true," she said, in that thick, rich, caky voice; "every good little boy and gell's to have a bun. Now then," she added, in a perfect blaze of tactlessness, "three cheers for the bride and bridegroom, and many happy returns."

The two had to stand side by side and hear those shrill, thin cheers, strengthened by the voices of fathers and mothers at the windows. He had to wave his hat to the crowd and to be waved at in return from every window in the street—even those too far away for their occupants to have any certain idea why they cheered and waved. She had to bow and kiss her hand to the children and to bow and smile to the window-dwellers.

Next moment she was out of the shop and running like a deer along a side-street, he following. They took hands and ran; and by luck their street brought them to a road where trams were, and escape. They rode on the top of the tram, and she held his hand all the way to Charing Cross. I cannot explain this. Neither of them spoke a word. Further, it was almost without a word that they got themselves to Richmond. It was not till they had been for many minutes in the deep quiet of the bracken and green leafage that she spoke, with a little laugh that had more than laughter in it.

"We might almost as well," she said, "have been married in church."

XIII

WARWICK

ONLY those who have gone through the ceremony of a mock marriage, from the gentlest motives, and have soothed the solicitude of a beloved and invalid aunt by the gift of the marriage certificate thus obtained, can have any idea of the minor difficulties which beset the path of the really unselfish. Had the ceremony been one in which either party was deceived as to its real nature the sequent embarrassments would have been far less. The first and greatest was the question of names. The persons mentioned in the certificate now bedewed by the joyful tears of the invalid aunt, and scorched by the fierce fires of a first-class family row, were committed, so far as the family and the world knew, to a wedding-journey. That is to say, Mr. and Mrs. Basingstoke, after posting the certificate, were to proceed on their honeymoon. But cold mock marriages claim no honeymoon. So far the only explanation of the relations of the now mockly married had been made to Mr. Schultz across the peaches in the sunned and shadowy arbor at Tunbridge Wells. To Mr. Schultz the two were brother and sister. To travel as Mr. and Mrs. Basingstoke presented difficulties almost insurmountable—to pursue their wanderings as Mr. and Miss Basingstoke involved bother about letters and the constant risk of explanations to any of the friends and relations of either across whose path fate might be spiteful enough to drive them. Because, of course, your friends and relations know how many brothers and sisters you have and what they look like, and those sort of people never forget. You could never persuade them that the young man with whom you were traveling was a brother whom they had overlooked or forgotten.

A long silence in the train that meant to go to Warwick was spent by each in the same tangle of puzzle and conjecture. They had the carriage to themselves. Her eyes were on the green changing picture framed by the window; his eyes noted the firm, pretty line of her chin, the way her hair grew, the delicate charm of the pale roses under the curve of her hat-brim—the proud carriage of head and neck; he liked the way she held herself, the way her hands lay in her lap, the self-possession and self-respect that showed in every line of that gracious figure.

THE INCREDIBLE HONEYMOON

The four walls of the carriage seemed to shut them in with a new and deeper intimacy than yesterday's. He would have liked to hold her hand as he had held it on the way to Richmond—to have her shoulder lightly touching his and to sit by her and watch the changing of that green picture from which she never turned her eyes. And all the time the two alternatives seesawed at the back of his mind: "Mr. and Mrs. or Mr. and Miss?"

Her eyes suddenly left the picture and met his. In that one glance she knew what sort of thoughts had been his, and knew also quite surely and unmistakably, as women do know such things, that the relations between them had been changed by that mock marriage—that now it would not be he who would make the advances. That he was hers for the asking, she knew, but she also knew that there would have to be asking, and that asking hers. She knew then, as well as she knew it later, that that act had set a barrier between them and that his would never be the hand to break it down; a barrier strong as iron, behind which she could, if she would, remain alone forever—and yet a barrier which, if she chose that it should be so, her choice could break at a touch, as bubbles are broken. She felt as perhaps a queen in old romance might have felt traveling through the world served only by a faithful knight. That they had held each other's hand on their wedding-day had been an accident. This would never happen again—unless she made it happen.

"We must have our letters sent to the post-offices where we go," she said, suddenly, turning to the problem at the back of her mind. "Then the aunts can call me 'Mrs.' when they write to me. I suppose they'll want to *call* me that?"

"Mrs. Basingstoke," he said, slowly. "Yes, it seems likely that they *will* want to."

"Then," she went on, "we needn't pretend to the hotel people that we're married. They'd be sure to find out we weren't, or something, and we should always be trembling on the perilous edge of detection. I couldn't bear to be always wondering whether the landlord had found us out."

"It would be intolerable," he agreed, deeply conscious of the admirable way in which she grasped this delicate nettle. "Whereas . . ."

"Whereas if we're Mr. and Miss Basingstoke at our hotels, and Mr. and Mrs. at the post-office, it's all as simple as the Hebrew alphabet."

"The Hebrew . . .?"

"Well, it's not quite as simple as A B C, but very nearly. So that's settled."

"What," he asked, hastily, anxious to show his sense of a difficulty avoided, a subject dismissed—

"what do you think about when you look out of the windows in trains? Or don't you think at all—just let the country flow through your soul as though it were music?"

"One does that when one's *in* it," she answered, "in woods and meadows and in those deep lanes where you see nothing but the hedges and the cart-tracks—and on the downs—yes. But when you look out at the country it's different, isn't it? One looks at the churches and thinks about all the people who were christened and married and buried there, and then you look at the houses they lived in—the old farm-houses more than anything. Do you know, all my life I've wished I'd been born a farmer's daughter. All the little things of life in those thatched homesteads are beautiful to me. The smell of the wood smoke, and the way all your life is next door to out-of-doors—always having to go out and feed the calves or the pigs or the fowls, and always little young things, the goslings and the ducklings and the chicks—you know how soft and pretty they are. And all these lovely little live things dependent on you. And the men as well—they come home tired from their work and you have their meals all ready—the bread you've baked yourself, and the pasties you've made—perhaps, even, you brew the beer and salt the pork—and they come in, your husband and your father and your brothers, and they think what a good housekeeper you are, and love you for it. Or if you're a man yourself, all your work's out of doors with the nice, clean earth and making things grow, and seeing the glorious seasons go round and round like a splendid kaleidoscope; and in the winter coming home through the dusk and seeing the dancing light of your own hearth-fire showing through the windows, till you go into the warm, cozy place, and then the red curtains are drawn and the door is shut, and you're safe inside—at home."

He felt in every word a new intimacy, a new confidence. For the first time she was speaking to him from the heart without afterthought and without reservations. And he knew why. He knew that the queen, confident and confiding, spoke to the faithful knight. And the matter of her speech no less than its manner enchanted him so that he could think of nothing better to say than:

"Go on—tell me some more."

"There isn't any more, only I think that must have been the life I lived in my last incarnation, because a little house in the country—any little house, even an old turnpike cottage—always seems to call out to me, 'Here I am! Come home! What a long time you've been away!'"

THE INCREDIBLE HONEYMOON

"And yet," he said, and felt, as he said it, how stupid he was being—"and yet you love traveling and adventure—seeing the world and the wonders of the world."

"Ah!" she said, "that's my new incarnation. But what the old one loved goes deeper than that. I love adventure and new bits of the world as I love strawberries and ice-cream, and waltzing and Chopin, but the little house in the green country is like the daily bread of the heart."

"I understand you," he said, slowly. "I understand you in the only possible way. I mean that's the way I feel about it, too. If you were really my sister, what a united family the last of the Basingstokes would be."

"Do you really feel the same about it—you, too?" she asked. "Oh, what a pity I wasn't born Basingstoke, and we would have lived on our own farm and been happy all our lives."

He would not say what he might have said, and her heart praised him for not saying it. And so at last they came to Warwick, and Charles had bounded from the dog-box all pink tongue and white teeth and strenuous white-covered muscles, and knocked down a little boy in a blue jersey, who had to be consoled by chocolate which came out of the machine like the god in the Latin tag. And then all the luggage was retrieved—there was

WARWICK

getting to be a most respectable amount of it, as she pointed out—and it and they and Charles got into a fly (for there are still places where an open carriage bears that ironic name) and drove through the afternoon sunshine to the Warwick Arms. But when they were asked to write their names in the visitors' book, each naturally signed a Christian name, and the management, putting two and two together, deduced Mr. and Mrs. Basingstoke, and entered this result in more intimate books, living in retirement in the glass case which preserves the young lady who knows all about which rooms you can have. The chambermaid and the boots agreed that Mr. and Mrs. Basingstoke were a handsome couple. Also, when a new-comer, signing his name, asked a question about the signatures just above his, "Mr. and Mrs. Basingstoke," was the answer he got.

Now all this time, for all her frankness, she had been concealing something from him.

You must know that the wedding-dinner, if a mock marriage can be said to involve a wedding-dinner, had been at the Star and Garter, and after the wooded slopes and the shining spaces of the river her London hotel had seemed but a dull and dusty resting-place. And it was she who had met him when he called to take her out to breakfast with a petition for more river. So they had taken

THE INCREDIBLE HONEYMOON

more river, in the shape of a Sunday at Coohmah, where the beautiful woods lean down to the water, and the many boats keep to the stream and the few creep into backwaters whither the swans follow you, and eat all the lunch if you will only give them half a chance. It was a delightful day, full of incident and charm. The cool, gleaming river, the self-possessed gray poplars, the generous, green-spreading beeches, the lovelorn willows trailing their tresses in the stream, the reeds and the rushes, the quiet, emphasized by the knowledge that but for the supremest luck they might have been two in a very large and noisy party, such as that on the steam-launch which thrust its nose into their backwater and had to back out with fussings and snortings, like a terrier out of a rabbit-hole. The dappled shadows on the spread carpet of lily-leaves, the green gleams in the deep darkness of the woods, the slow, dripping veil of dusk through which they rowed slowly back to the inn—even being late for the train and having to run for it—all, as he said, when they had caught the train and were crammed into a first-class carriage with three boating-men, a painted lady, an aged beau, and a gentleman almost of color, from Brazil—all had been very good. But he did not know all. There had been a moment, while he had gone in to the bar of the inn to settle for the boat—a moment in which she waited in the little grassy garden that shelves down to the river's edge—and in that moment a boat slid up to the landing-stage. The first man to get out of it was nobody, and didn't matter. The second was Mr. Schultz. As it happened, her face was lighted by a yellow beam from one of the inn windows, and as he landed the beam from the other window fell across his face, so that they saw and recognized each other in a blaze of light that might have been arranged for no other purpose.

He raised his cap and she saw that he meant to speak, but one of his companions thrust the painter into his hand at exactly the nick of time. He was held there, for the moment. She had the sense to walk slowly into the inn, and Mr. Schultz might well have thought that she was staying there. She meant him to think so. Anyhow, he did not cast the painter from him, as he might have done, and hurry after her. "Later on will do," was what his attitude and his look expressed.

The moment she was out of his sight she quickened her pace, found Mr. Edward Basingstoke in the bar putting his change in his pocket, and, the moment the two were outside the street door, said, just, "We must run for it." This was, providentially, true. And they ran for it, just catching it, without a breath to spare.

THE INCREDIBLE HONEYMOON

Why did she not tell him that she had seen Schultz, that stout squire of the South Coast road? For one thing, Mr. Schultz seemed long ago and irrelevant. For another, he was discordant, and his very name, spoken, would break the spell of a very charming quiet which had infolded her and Edward all day long. Then there was the crowded carriage with the Brazilian gentleman, all observant, black, beady eye, and long yellow ear. And then, anyhow, what was the good of raking up Mr. Schultz, whom Edward had never really liked. So she did not tell him. Nor, for much the same reason, did he tell her that one of that shouting party who climbed into the train after it had actually started, and whom he saw as he leaned out of the window to buy chocolate from an accidental boy, was very like that chap Schultz —as like, in fact, as two peas.

And the next day she packed up everything, and he packed up a good deal, and they started for Warwick; arrived there, had luncheon, and became immediately a pair of ardent sight-seers.

The guide-book in the coffee-room assured them that "no visitor to Warwick with any sense of propriety thinks of remaining long without paying his respects to that historic and majestic pile known as Warwick Castle," and this, they agreed, settled the question.

WARWICK

So they went and saw Warwick Castle, with its great gray towers and its high gray walls, its green turf, and old, old trees. They saw the banqueting-hall that was burned down, and Guy's punch-bowl that holds Heaven knows how many gallons.

"It makes you thirsty to look at it," said Edward.

Also they saw the Portland vase which lives in a glass house all by itself, and the bed where Queen Anne slept, and the cedar drawing-room and the red drawing-room and the golden drawing-room, and all the other rooms which are "shown to visitors," and longed lawlessly to see the rooms that are not so shown.

"There must be *some* comfortable rooms in the house," she said. "Even lords and ladies and Miss O'Gradys couldn't really live in these museums." And, indeed, all the rooms they saw were much too full of things curious, precious, beautiful, and ugly; but mostly large and all costly.

"It must be pretty awful to be as rich as all this," said Edward, as they came out of the castle gate.

"Would it be? The guide-books say Lady Warwick says she strives to fulfil, imperfectly, it may be, the duties of her stewardship and the privileges of her heritage. It would be interesting, don't you think, to find out just exactly what those were?"

"If I had a castle," said he, "there shouldn't be a knickknack in it, nor a scrap of furniture later than seventeen hundred."

"I sometimes wonder whether it's fair," she said, "the way we collect old things. Have you noticed that poor people's houses haven't a decent bit of furniture in them? When my mother was little the cottages used to have old bureaus and tables and chests that had come down from father to son and from mother to daughter."

"It's true," said he, "and the worst of it is that we've not only taken away their furniture, but we've taken away their taste for it. They prefer plush and machine-made walnut to the old oak and elm and beech and apple-wood. It would be no good to give them back their old furnishing unless we could give them back their love of it. And that we can't do."

"But if we bought modern things?"

"Even then they wouldn't care for the old ones. And the only beautiful modern things we have are imitations of the old ones. We've lost the art of furniture-making, and the art of architecture, and we're losing even the art of life. It's getting to be machine-made, like our chair-legs and our stone facings. I sometimes wonder whether we are really on the down-grade—and whether the grade is so steep that we sha'n't be able to stop—and go on till there's no life possible except the life that's represented by the plush and walnut at one end and motors and the Ritz at the other."

"Can't we resist? all the people who still care for beautiful things?"

"We can collect them; it's not taking them from the poor now—it's taking them from the dealers who have cleared out the farms and cottages and little houses. I suppose one might make a nest, and live in it, but that wouldn't change things or stop the uglification of everything. You can't make people live beautifully by act of Parliament. The impulse to make and own beautiful things has to come from within—and it seems as though it were dead—killed by machinery and *laissez-faire* and the gospel of individualism, and I'm sorry to talk like a Fabian tract, but there it is. Forgive me, and let's go down to Guy's Cliff and see the Saxon Mill and the perfect beauty of mixed architecture that wasn't trying to imitate anything."

"Yes, but go on with the tract."

"There isn't any more, except that what's so difficult is to know how to live without hurting some one else. This is my wander year. I'm spending my money just now for fun and to have a good time. I feel I deserve a holiday and I'm

THE INCREDIBLE HONEYMOON

taking one. But what's one to do with one's life? How can one use one's money so as to do no harm?"

"If you invest it in mines or factories or railways, doesn't that employ people and make trade better?" she asked, diffidently. "I'm sure I've heard people say so."

"Yes," he said, grimly, "so have I. And, of course, it's true. You launch your money into this horrible welter of hard work and chancy wages, and it helps to keep some people in motors and fur coats and champagne and diamonds, and it helps, too, to keep others on the perilous edge of despair, to keep them alive in a world where they're never sure of next week's meals, never free from worry from the cradle to the grave, with no poetry in their lives but love, and no magic but drink."

"But what are we to do?" she asked, and they paused a moment on the bridge to look to the splendid mass of Warwick Castle along the river where the swans float and the weeping willows trail their hair in the water.

"I wish I knew," he said. "There must be some way to live without having any part in the muddle."

"We'll find a way," said she. And his heart leaped, for he knew that this was the most intimate thing she had ever said to him.

XIV

STRATFORD-ON-AVON

WHEN you have seen Warwick Castle and Guy's Cliff and the Saxon Mill—which is so old that it must be soothing to the most tempestuous temperament—and you hasten back to your hotel and get your dog—if that dog be Charles—on purpose to expose him to its calm influences, you go to St. Mary's Church, which is, the guide-book tells you, "one of the most remarkable specimens of ecclesiastical architecture extant," and you see the Norman Crypt, and the clumsy sarcophagus of Fulke Greville, Lord Brooke, who wrote his own epitaph, and you read how he was "servant to Queen Elizabeth, Canceller to King James, and friend to Sir Philip Sidney."

Also you see the Beauchamp Chapel, and love it and linger in it, admiring the tombs of the earls of Warwick and other grown-ups, and feeling, even after all these years, a thrill of sadness at the sight of the little effigy of the child whose brocaded gown the marble so wonderfully produces and whose little years knock at your heart for pity.

"Here resteth," says the monument, "the body of the noble Impe Robert of Dudley, . . . a child of greate parentage, but of farre greater hope and towardness, taken from this transitory unto the everlasting life in his tender age, . . . on Sunday the 19 of July, in the yeare of our Lorde God 1584."

You see, also, the Warwick pew, and wish you could have worshiped there.

Then you go to Leicester's Hospital, half timbered and beautiful, with the row of whispering limes on its terraced front, where the "brethren" still wear the "gown of blew stuff with the badge of the bear and ragged staff on the left sleeve." And the badges are still those provided by Lord Leicester in 1571.

You are sorry that the old banqueting-hall should now be used for the coal-cellar and the laundry of the brethren, and still more sorry that the minstrels' gallery should have been cut off to enlarge the drawing-room of the Master's house. If you are of a rude and democratic nature you may possibly comment on this in audible voices beneath the Master's windows, which, I am sorry to say, was what Mr. Basingstoke and his companion did.

STRATFORD-ON-AVON

You will see the Sidney porcupine on the wall of the quadrangle, some gilded quills missing, and no wonder, after all these years. You will see— and perhaps neglect to reverence, as they did—the great chair once occupied by that insufferable monarch and prig, James the First. You will visit the Brethren's Chapel, which seems to be scented by all the old clothes ever worn by any of the old brethren, and you will come out again into the street, and, as you cross the threshold, it will be like stepping across three hundred years, and you will say so. Then you will probably say, "What about Stratford for this afternoon?" At least, that is what Edward said. And as he said it he was aware of a figure in black which said,

"Can you tell me the way to Droitwich?"

It was a woman, spare and pale, in black that was green, but brushed to threadbareness.

"Do you want to walk?" Edward asked.

"I've got to, sir," she said.

"Do you mind," he asked, "telling me why you want to go?"

"I've got relations there, sir," said the woman in black, raising to his the plaintive blue eyes of a child set in a face that fifty years and more had wrinkled like a February apple. "My husband's relations, that is. They might do something to help me. I might be able to be of use to them, just to work out my keep. It isn't much I require. But I couldn't—"

She stopped, and Edward Basingstoke knew that she couldn't even bring herself to name the great terror of the poor—the living tomb which the English call the workhouse.

"I'm afraid you've had a hard time," said Mr. Basingstoke.

"I had many happy days," she said, simply. "I always think you pay for everything you have, sooner or later. And I'm paying now. I don't grudge it, but I'd like to end respectable. And thank you for asking so kindly, sir, and now I'll be getting on." And he saw in her eyes the fear that he would offer her money to pay her way to Droitwich.

Instead he said: "We're motoring your way this afternoon. If you'll let us give you a lift—"

The woman looked from one to the other. "Well," she said, "I do call that kind. But I wasn't asking for any help. And I'd best be getting on."

Then the other woman came quite close to the woman in black. "Won't you," she said, "come and have dinner with us—and then we'll drive you over? Do come. We're so happy and we do hate to think that you aren't. Perhaps we can think of some way to help you . . . find you some work or something," she added, hastily, answering the protest in the blue eyes.

"I don't like to, miss," she said, "thanking you all the same. It's truly good of you—but—"

Edward moved away a pace or two and lit a cigarette. He never knew what his lady said to the woman in black, but when he turned again a handkerchief was being restored to a rubbed black leather reticule and the woman in black was saying,

"Well, ma'am, since you say that, of course I can't say no, and thank you kindly."

The three had dinner together in the little private room over the porch at the Warwick Arms, and as they passed through the hall there could have been, for the little woman in black, no better armor against the sniffs of chambermaids and the cold eyes of the lady in the glass case than the feel of another woman's hand on her arm. She was very silent and shy, but not awkward or clumsy, during the meal, and when it was finished Edward got up and said,

"Well, Katherine, I'll leave you two to talk things over."

It was the first time he had called her by her name. She flushed and sparkled, and was startled and amazed next moment to know that she had answered,

"Yes, dear, do—"

THE INCREDIBLE HONEYMOON

Edward, however, was not unduly elated. He knew how women will play the part set for them, to the least detail. She hoped he had not noticed the slip which, quite unconsciously, the opening of her heart toward this sad sister-woman had led her to make. He wished that she had not first called him that in a mere desire to act up to what this woman would expect.

He left them, and then the pitiful little story all came out, with fit accompaniment of sighs, and presently tears, together with those sweet and tender acts and words which blend with the sighs and tears of the sorrowful into a melody as sad as beautiful. They had been married thirty-seven years next Michaelmas; they had had a little shop—a little needlework and fancy shop. She had done well enough with the customers, but he had always done the buying, and when he was taken . . .

"Ah, my dear, don't cry," said the one who was young and happy, "don't cry. You'll make him so sad."

"Do you think he knows?" the widow asked.

"Of course he knows. He knows everything's going to be all right, only he hates to see you miserable. *He* knows it's only a little time, really, before you and he will be together again, and happy for ever and ever."

"I wish I could believe that."

"You must, because it's true. I expect he's been praying for you, and that's why you met us —because, you know, I'm certain my"— she hesitated, but the word came instead of "brother," which was what she thought she meant to say— "my husband will think of something for you to do to earn your living; he's so clever. And I suppose the business—"

Yes. The business had gone to pieces. Fashions change so, and the widow had not known how to follow the fashions in needlework. There was only enough left to pay the creditors, but every one *had* been paid, and with the pound or two left over she had lived, trying to get needle work, or even, at last, charring or washing. But it had all been no good; nothing had been any good.

"And now," said Katherine, "everything's going to be good. You'll see. Edward will think of something. Don't cry any more. You must not cry. I can't bear it, dear. Don't."

"I'm only crying for joy," said the woman whose life was over. "Even if he doesn't think of anything, I can't ever despair again, and you being like you have to me."

But when Edward came back he had thought of something. His old nurse, it seemed, was in temporary charge of a house that wanted a housekeeper, and he was sure Mrs. Burbidge understood housekeeping.

Mrs. Burbidge owned to an understanding of plain cooking and plain housekeeping. Also needlework, both the plain and the fine. "But not where butlers are kept," she said, apprehensively.

"This is a farm-house," said Edward. "Not a butler within miles."

"My father was a farmer, in Somerset," said Mrs. Burbidge, "but, oh, sir, you don't know anything about me. Suppose I was a fraud like you read of in the newspapers. But the vicar at home would speak for me."

"Your face speaks for you," said Katherine, and within half an hour all was settled—the old nurse telegraphed to, money found for such modest outfit as even a farmer's housekeeper must have, the train fixed that should take the widow to London, the little hotel named where she should spend a night, and the train decided on that should take her in the morning to the farm-house that needed a housekeeper.

"It's no use me saying anything," said Mrs. Burbidge, at parting, "but—"

"There's nothing to say," said Katherine, and kissed her, "only you will write to the Reverend

Smilie at Eccles vicarage. I can't be easy unless you do," were her last words.

When she was gone they stood a moment looking at each other, and each would have liked to hold out hands to the other, to come quite close in the ecstasy of a kind deed jointly done. Instead of which he said, awkwardly:

"I suppose that was a thoroughly silly thing to do."

And she answered, "Oh, well, let's hope it will turn out all right."

An interchange which left both of them chilled and a little disenchanted.

It was Edward who had the sense to say, as the motor whirled them toward Stratford, "That was all nonsense, you know, that we said just now."

She was disingenuous enough to say, "What—"

"About Mrs. Burbidge perhaps not being all right. She's as right as rain. I don't know what made me say it."

"A sort of 'do-good-by-stealth-and-blush-to-find it-fame' feeling, I expect, wasn't it? Of course she's all right. You know I knew you knew she was, don't you?"

"I know now," said he. "Yes, of course I knew it. Don't let's pretend we aren't both jolly glad we met her."

"No, don't let's," said she. And laid her hand

THE INCREDIBLE HONEYMOON

on his. His turned under it and held it, lightly yet tenderly, as his hand knew that hers would wish to be held, and not another word did either say till their car drew up at the prosperous, preposterous Shakespeare Inn at Stratford-on-Avon. But all through the drive soft currents of mutual kindness and understanding, with other electricities less easy to classify, ran from him to her and from her to him, through the contact of their quiet clasped hands.

The inn at Stratford is intolerably half timbered. Whatever there may have been of the old woodwork is infinitely depreciated by the modern imitation which flaunts itself everywhere. The antique mockery is only skin deep and does not extend to the new rooms, each named after one of Shakespeare's works, and all of a peculiarly unpleasing shape, and furnished exactly like the rooms of any temperance hotel. The room where Katherine washed the dust of the road from her pretty face was called "The Tempest," and the sitting-room where they had tea was a hideous oblong furnished in the worst taste of the middle-Victorian lower middle class, and had "Hamlet" painted on its door.

"We must see the birthplace, I suppose," said Edward, "but before we go I should like to warn you that there is not a single authentic relic of

Shakespeare, unless it's the house where they say he was born, and even that was never said to be his birthplace till a hundred and fifty years after his death, and even then two other houses claimed the same honor. If ever a man was born in three places at once, like a bird, that man was William Shakespeare."

"You aren't a Baconian, are you?" she asked, looking at him rather timidly across the teacups. "But you can't be, because I know they're all mad."

"A good many of them are very, very silly," he owned, "but don't be afraid. I'm not a Baconian, for Baconians are convinced that Bacon wrote the whole of Elizabethan and Jacobean literature off his own bat. I only think there's a mystery. You remember Dickens said the life of Shakespeare was a fine mystery and he trembled daily lest something should turn up."

"And nothing has."

"Nothing. That's just it. There's hardly anything known about the man. He was born here—died here. He went to London and acted. One of his contemporaries says that the top of his performance was the Ghost in 'Hamlet.' He married, he had children, he got hold of money enough to buy a house, he got a coat of arms, he lent money and dunned people for it, he speculated in

THE INCREDIBLE HONEYMOON

corn, he made a will in which he mentions neither his plays nor his books, but is very particular about his second-best bed and his silver-gilt bowl. He died, and was buried. That's all that's known about him. I'm not a Baconian, Princess, but I'm pretty sure that whoever wrote 'Hamlet,' that frowzy, money-grubbing provincial never did."

"But we'll go and see his birthplace, all the same, won't we?" she said.

And they went.

If she desired to worship at the shrine of Shakespeare he did not give her much chance. She listened to the talk of the caretaker, but always he was at her ear with the tale of how often Shakespeare's chair had been sold and replaced by a replica, how the desk shown as his is that of an eighteenth-century usher and not of a sixteenth-century scholar. How the ring engraved "W. S." was found in the surface of the ground, near the church, in 1810, where, one supposes, it had lain unnoticed since Shakespeare dropped it there two hundred years before.

At the grammar-school Edward pointed out that there is no evidence to show that Shakespeare ever attended this or any other school. Anne Hathaway's cottage could not be allowed to be Anne Hathaway's, since it was only in 1770 that

STRATFORD-ON-AVON

its identity was fixed on, two other houses having previously shared the honor. Like her husband, she would seem to have possessed the peculiar gift of being born in three places at once.

"I don't think I like it," she said at last. "I'd rather believe everything they say. It's such a very big lot of lies, if they are lies. Let's go to the church. The man's grave's his own, I suppose."

"I suppose so," said he, but not with much conviction; "anyhow, I won't bore you with any more of the stuff. But it *is* a fine mystery, and there's a corner of me that would like to live in Bloomsbury and grub among books all day at the British Mu. and half the night in my booky little den, and see if I couldn't find something out. But the rest of me wants different things, out-of-door things, and things that lead to something more than finding the key to a door locked three hundred years ago."

The bust of Shakespeare in Stratford Church is a great blow to the enthusiast. A stubby, sensual, Dutch-looking face.

"I wish they'd been content with the gravestone," she said, and read aloud the words:

> "Goodfrend for Jesus sake forbeare
> To digg the dust encloasèd heare
> Blest be ye man yt spares these stones
> And curst be he yt moves my bones."

"There's not much chance of any one doing that—look, the altar-step goes right across the tombstone. I wonder what they *would* find, if they *did* move the stone."

"Nothing, madam," said a voice behind her—"nothing human, that is."

She turned to face a tall, gaunt man in loose, ill-fitting clothes with a despatch-case in one hand and three or four note-books in the other. "Excuse my joining in," he said, "but I couldn't help hearing what you said. Whatever there is in that tomb, there is not the body of the man Shakespeare. Manuscripts there may be, but no corpse."

"What makes you think so?" she asked.

"Evidence, madam, evidence. The evidence of facts as well as of ciphers."

"Oh," she said, and smiled brilliantly, "you must be a Baconian. How very interesting!"

Now she had received all Edward's criticisms of Shakespearian legend with a growing and visible impatience. Yet for this stranger she had nothing but sympathy and interest.

"It *is* interesting," said the stranger. "There's nothing like it. I've spent eighteen years on it, and I know now how little I know. It isn't only Bacon and Shakespeare; it's a great system—a great cipher system extending through all the great works of the period."

STRATFORD-ON-AVON

"But what is it that you hope to find out in the end?" she asked. "Secrets of state, or the secret of the philosopher's stone, or what?"

"The truth," he said, simply. "There's nothing else worth looking for. The truth, whatever it is. To follow truth, no matter where it leads. I'd go on looking, even if I thought that at the end I should find that that Stratford man did write the plays." He looked up contemptuously at the smug face of the bust.

"It's a life's work," said Mr. Basingstoke, "and I should think more than one life's work. Do you find that you can bring your mind to any other kind of work?"

"I gave up everything else," said the stranger. "I was an accountant, and I had some money and I'm living on it. But now . . . now I shall have to do something else. I've got a situation in London. I'm going there next week. It's the end of everything for me."

"There ought to be some endowment for your sort of research," said Edward.

"Of course there ought," said the man, eagerly, "but people don't care. The few who do care don't want the truth to come out. They want to keep that thing"— he pointed to the bust—"to keep that thing enthroned on its pedestal forever. It pays, you see. Great is Diana of the Ephesians."

"I suppose it wouldn't need to be a very handsome endowment. I mean that sort of research work can be done at museums. You don't have to buy the books," Edward said.

"A lot can be done with libraries, of course. But I have a few books—a good few. I should like to show them to you some day—if you're interested in the subject."

"I am," said Edward, with a glance at the girl, "or I used to be. Anyhow, I should like very much to see your books. You have a Du Bartas, of course?"

"Three," said the stranger, "and six of the Sylva Sylvarum, and Argalus and Perthenia—do you know that—Quarles—and—"

Next moment the two men were up to the eyes in a flood of names, none of which conveyed anything to her. But she saw that Edward was happy. At the same time, the hour was latish. She waited for the first pause—a very little one—but she drove the point of her wedge into it sharply.

"Wouldn't it be nice if you were to come back to dinner with us, at Warwick, then we should have lots of time to talk."

"I was going to London to-night," said the stranger, "but if Warwick can find me a night's lodging I shall only too gladly avail myself of your gracious invitation, Mrs.—"

"Basingstoke," said Edward.

The stranger had produced a card and she read on it:

>Dr. C. P. Vandervelde,
>Ohio College, U. S. A.

"Yes," he said, "I'm an American. I think almost all serious Baconians are. I hope you haven't a prejudice against my country, Mrs. Basingstoke—"

"It's Miss Basingstoke," she said, thinking of the hotel, "and I've never met an American that I didn't like."

He made her a ceremonious and old-fashioned bow. "Inscrutable are the ways of fate," he said. "Only this morning I was angry because the chambermaid at my inn in Birmingham destroyed my rubbing of the grave inscription, and I had to come to Stratford to get another. Yes, I could have written, but it was so near, and I shall soon be chained to an office desk—and now, in this of all spots, I meet youth and beauty and sympathy and hospitality. It is an omen."

"And what," she asked, as they paced down the church, "was the cipher that said there was nothing in the tomb? Or would you rather not talk about your ciphers?"

"I desire nothing better than to talk of them,"

he answered. "It's the greatest mistake to keep these things secret. We ought all to tell all we know—and if we all did that and put together the little fragment of knowledge we have gathered, we should soon piece together the whole puzzle. The first words I found on the subject are, 'Reader, read all, no corpse lies in this tomb,' and so on, and with the same letters another anagram in Latin, beginning *'Lector intra sepulcho jacet nullum cadaver.'* I'll show you how I got it when we're within reach of a table and light."

They lingered a moment on the churchyard terrace where the willows overhang the Avon and the swans move up and down like white-sailed ships.

"How hospitable we're getting," she said to Edward that night when their guest had gone to his humbler inn—"two visitors in one day!"

"Katherine," he said, just for the pleasure of saying it, for they two were alone, so he could not have been speaking to any one else—"Katherine, that man's ciphers are wonderful. And what a gift of the gods—to possess an interest that can never fail and that costs nothing for its indulgence, not like postage-stamps or orchids or politics or racing!"

"The ciphers were wonderful," she said. "I had no idea such things were possible. I understood quite a lot," she added, a little defiantly. "But it's rather hateful to think of his being chained to a desk doing work that isn't *his* work."

"That, or something like it, is the lot of most people," he said, "but it needn't be his lot. It's for you to say. I can very well afford a small endowment for research, if you say so."

"But why must *I* decide?"

"Because," he said, slowly, "I felt when I was talking to you to-day that you hated everything I said; you wanted to go on believing in all the Shakespeare legends."

"I think I said so. I'm not sure that I meant it. Anyhow, if it rests with me I say give him his research endowment, if he'll take it."

"He'll take it. I'll get a man I know at Balliol to write, offering it. In his beautiful transatlantic simplicity the dear chap will think the college is offering the money. He'll take it like a lamb. But won't you tell me—why was it that you hated me to be interested in this business and you are glad that this Vandervelde should be helped to go on with it?"

"I should like him to be happy," she said, "and there's nothing else in life for him—he has given up everything else for it. I want him, at least, to have the treasure he's paid everything for—the joy of his work. But that sort of joy should be reserved for the people who can have nothing else. But for you—well, somehow, I feel that people who take up a thing like this ought to be prepared to sacrifice everything else in life to it, as he has done. And I could not bear that you should do it. Life has so much besides for you."

"Yes," he said, "life holds very much for me."

"And for me, too," she said, and with that gave him her hand for good night.

He was certain afterward that it had not been his doing, and yet it must have been, for her hand had not moved in his. And yet he had found it laid not against his lips, but against his cheek, and he had held it there in silence for more than a moment before she drew it away and said good night.

At the door she turned and looked back over her shoulder. "Good night," she said again. "Good night, Edward."

And that was the first time she called him by his name.

XV

KENILWORTH

THERE are some very pleasant shops in Warwick, and if you have time and no money you can spend some very agreeable mornings wandering from one shop to another, asking the prices of things you have all the will but none of the means to buy. If you have money and time you will buy a few of the things whose prices you have asked. Edward bought a ring, crystal with brilliants around it, very lovely and very expensive, and some topazes set in old silver, quite as beautiful but not so dear.

Then they went to the old-furniture shops, where he excited the vexed admiration of the dealers by his unerring eye for fakes. He bought an oak chest, carved with a shield of arms, the date 1612, and the initials "I. B."

"If we were really married," he told her, "I should be vandal enough to alter that 'I' to make it stand for your name."

THE INCREDIBLE HONEYMOON

"I should not think it a vandal's act—if we were married," she answered, and their eyes met. He bought tables and chairs of oak and beech; a large French cupboard whose age, he said, made it a fit mate for the chest; he bought a tall clock with three tarnished gold pines atop, and some brass pots and pewter plates. She strayed away from him at the last shop, while he was treating for a Welsh dresser with brass handles, and when he had made his bargain he followed her, to find her lovingly fingering chairs of *papier-mâché* painted with birds and flowers and inlaid with mother-of-pearl. There was a table, too, graceful and gay as the chairs, and a fire-screen of fine needlework.

"You hate anything that isn't three or four hundred years old," she said. "It's dreadful that our tastes don't agree, isn't it? Don't you think we ought to part at once? 'They separated on account of incompatibility of furniture.'"

"But don't you like the things we have been getting?"

"Of course I do, but I like these, too. They're like lavender and pot-pourri, and ladies who had still-rooms and made scents and liqueurs and confections in them, and walked in their gardens in high-heeled shoes and peach-blossom petticoats."

"Why not buy them, then?"

KENILWORTH

"I would if I had a house. If I were buying things I should first buy everything I liked, and not try to keep to any particular period. I believe the things would all settle down and be happy together if you loved them all. Did you get your precious dresser? And are you going to buy that Lowestoft dessert-service to go on it?"

He bought the Lowestoft dessert-service, beautiful with red, red roses and golden tracery; and next day he got up early and went around and bought all the painted mother-of-pearly things that she had touched. He gave the man an address in Sussex to which to send everything, and he wrote a long letter to his old nurse, whose address it was that he had given.

They had had dinner in the little private sitting-room over the front door, the smallest private room, I believe, that ever took an even semi-public part in the life of a hotel. It was quite full of curly glass vases and photographs in frames of silver and of plush, till Edward persuaded the landlady to remove them, "for fear," as he said, "we should have an accident and break any of them."

They breakfasted here, and here, too, luncheon was served, so that they met none of the other guests at meals, and in their in-goings and out-comings they only met strangers. Mr. Schultz might still have been at Tunbridge Wells, for any sense they had of him.

Presently and inevitably came the afternoon when they motored to Kenilworth.

"I've always wanted to see Kenilworth," she told him, "almost more than any place. Kenilworth and the Pyramids and Stonehenge and the Lost City in India—you know the one that the very name of it is forgotten, and they just found it by accident, all alone and beautiful, with panthers in it instead of people, and trees growing out of the roofs of the palaces, like Kipling's Cold Lairs."

"I get a sort of cold comfort from the thought of that city," he said. "That and Babylon and Nineveh and the great cities in Egypt. When I go through Manchester or New Cross or Sheffield I think, 'Some day grass and trees will cover up all this ugliness and flowers will grow again in the Old Kent Road.'"

"It is cold comfort," she said. "I wish flowers and grass could cover the ugliness, but I should like them to be flowers planted by us living people —not just wild flowers and the grass on graves."

The first sight of Kenilworth was naturally a great shock to her, as it always is to those who know of it only from books and photographs and engravings.

KENILWORTH

"Oh dear," she said, "how horrible! Why, it's pink!"

It is, bright pink, and to eyes accustomed to the dignified gray monochrome of our South Country castles, Bodiam and Hever, Pevensey and Arundel, Kenilworth at first seems like a bad joke, or an engraving colored by a child who has used up most of the paints in its paint-box and has had to make shift with Indian red and vermilion, the only two tints surviving. But when you get nearer, when you get quite near, when you look up at the great towers, when you walk between the great masses of it, and see the tower that Elizabeth's Leicester built, and the walls that Cromwell's soldiers battered down, you forgive Kenilworth for being pink, and even begin to admit that pink is not such a bad color for castles.

At Kenilworth you talk, of course, about Queen Elizabeth, and the one who has read the guide-books tells the one who hasn't that when the Queen visited Leicester he had a new bridge built over his lake so that she might enter the castle by a way untrodden by any previous guest. Also that during her visit the clock bell rang not a note and that the clock stood still withal, the hands of it pointing ever to two o'clock, the hour of banquet. Further, that during her visit of seventeen days Kenilworth Castle managed to put away three hundred and twenty hogsheads of beer.

"Those were great days," said Edward.

There are towers to climb at Kenilworth, as well as towers to gaze at, and with that passion for ascending steps which marks the young the two made their way to the top of one tower after another. It was as they leaned on the parapet of the third and looked out over the green country that Edward broke off in an unflattering anecdote of my Lord of Leicester. He stiffened as a pointer stiffens when it sees a partridge.

"Look!" he said, "look!"

Two fields away sheep were feeding—a moment ago calm, white shapes dotting a pastoral landscape, now roused to violent and unsuitable activities by the presence among them of some strange foe, some inspirer of the ungovernable fear that can find relief only in flight. The scurrying mass of them broke a little, and the two on the tower saw the shape of terror. They heard it, also. It was white and active. It barked.

"Oh, run," said she; "it *is* Charles. I'm almost certain it is. Oh, run!" And he turned and ran down the tower steps. She saw him come out and cross the grassy square of the castle at fine racing speed.

"It *is* Charles," she assured herself. "It must

be." Yet how could even that inspired dog have escaped from the stable at Warwick where they had left him, have followed their motor, and got here so soon. She could not know that another motor from the hotel, coming out to pick up a client, had overtaken Charles laboring up the hill from the top of which you get your first view of the castle towers, and, recognizing the dog—as who that had ever seen him could fail to do—had, so to speak, offered him a lift. Charles had accepted, and would have been handed over to his master's chauffeur at the Castle Gate House but that, a little short of that goal, as the car waited for a traction engine to pass it in the narrow way, Charles had seen the sheep, and with one bound of desperate gallantry was out and after them before his charioteer could even attempt restraint. And now Charles was in full pursuit of the sheep, barking happily in complete enjoyment of this thrilling game, and Edward was in pursuit of Charles, shouting as he ran. But Charles had no mind to listen—one could always pretend afterward that one had not heard, and no dog was more skilful than Charles in counterfeiting unconsciousness, nor in those acts of cajolery which soften the hearts of masters. His surprised delight when he should at last discover that his master was there and desired his company would be acted to the

THE INCREDIBLE HONEYMOON

life and would be enough to soften any heart. If either had looked up and back he could have seen a white speck on a red tower, which was Herself, watching the chase. But neither of them did. More observant and, to his own thinking, more fortunate, was another visitor to the castle; he, to be exact, whom what we may call Charles's motor had come to Kenilworth to pick up.

He had seen the fleecy scurrying, heard the yaps of pursuit, seen the flying form of Edward, and entered sufficiently into the feelings of Charles to be certain that the chase was not going to be a short one. He now saw from the foot of Mervyn's tower the white speck against blue sky. He made his way straight to the tower where she stood. She saw him crossing the grassy court which Edward's flying feet had but just now passed over. He came quickly and purposefully, and he was Mr. Schultz—none other.

Now she was not afraid of Mr. Schultz. Why should she be? He had been very kind, and of course she was not ungrateful, but it was a shock to see him there—a shock almost as great as that given by the pinkness of Kenilworth, and, anyhow, she did not want to meet him again; anyhow, not to-day; anyhow, not on the top of a tower. And it was quite plain to her that he had perceived her presence, had recognized her, and was coming

KENILWORTH

up expressly because of that—that his views were not hers, that he did want to meet her again, did want to meet her to-day, did want to meet her on top of a tower—this tower.

She looked around her "like a hunted thing," as they say, and then she remembered a very little room, hardly more than a recess, opening from the staircase. If she hurried down, hid there, and stood very close to the wall, he would pass by and not notice, and as he went up she could creep down and out, and, keeping close to the walls, get away toward Edward and Charles and the sheep and all the things that do not make for conversation with Mr. Schultz.

Lightly and swiftly as a hunted cat she fled down the stairs on whose lower marches was the sound of boots coming up toward her, echoing in the narrow tower like the tramp of an armed man. It came to her, as she reached the little room and stood there, her white gown crushed against the red stones, how a captive in just such a tower in the old days she and Edward had been talking of might have seized such a chance of escape from real and horrible danger, might have hidden as she was hiding, have held his breath as she now held hers, and how his heart would have beat, even as hers was beating, at the step of the guard coming toward the hiding-place, passing it, going on to

THE INCREDIBLE HONEYMOON

the tower-top while he, the fugitive, crept down toward liberty and sunlight and the good green world roofed with the good free sky.

The thought did not make for calmness. She said afterward that the tower must have been haunted by the very spirit of fear, for a panic terror came over her, something deeper and fiercer than anything Schultz could inspire—at any rate, in this century—and a caution and care that such as fear alone can teach. She slid from her hiding-place and down the stair, and as she went she heard above her those other steps, now returning. Nothing in the world seemed so good as the thought of the sunshine and free air into which in another moment she would come out. Round and round the spirals of the stone staircase went her noiseless, flying feet; the sound of the feet that followed came louder and quicker; a light showed at the bottom of the stairs; she rounded the last curve with a catch of the breath that was almost a cry, and in her eyes the vision of the fair, free outside world. She sprang toward green grass and freedom and sunlight, and four dark walls received her. For half-way down that tower the steps divide and she had passed the division and taken the stairs that led down past the level of the earth. And the light that had seemed to come through the doorway of the tower came through the high-set window of a dungeon, and there was no way out save by the stairs on which already she could hear feet descending. The man who followed her had not missed the way.

To turn back and meet that man on the stairs was impossible. She stood at bay. And she knew what the captive in old days must have felt—what the rabbit feels when it is caught in the trap. She stood rigid, with such an access of blind terror that the sight of the man, when he came down the last three steps, was almost—no, quite—relief. She had not fled from him, but from something more vague and more terrible. And when he spoke fear left her altogether, and she asked herself, "How could I have been so silly?"

"Miss Basingstoke?" He spoke on what he meant for a note of astonishment and pleasure, but his acting was not so good as hers, and he had to supplement it by adding, "This is, indeed, a delightful surprise."

"Oh, Mr. Schultz," she said, and quite gaily and lightly, too—"how small the world is! Of all unlikely places to meet any one one knows!" and she made to pass him and go up the stairs. But he stood square and firm at the stair-foot.

"No hurry," he said, "no hurry—since we *have* met. It is a wonderful pleasure to me, Miss

Basingstoke. Don't cut it short. And what have you been doing all this long time?"

"Oh, traveling about," she answered, watching the stair-foot as the rabbit from beside its burrow might watch the exit at which a terrier is posted. "Just seeing England, you know. We neglect England too much, don't you think, rushing off to the Riviera and Egypt and India and places like that when all the while there are the most beautiful things at home."

"I agree," he said, "the most beautiful things are in England," and lest his meaning should escape her, added, with a jerk of a bow, "and the most beautiful people." And still he stood there, smiling and not moving.

"Have you your car with you?" she asked, for something to say.

"No, but I'll send for it if you like. We could have some pleasant drives—Stratford, Shakespeare's birthplace—"

"We've been to Stratford," she put in, and went a step nearer to the stair-foot.

"Then anywhere you like. Shall I send for the car?"

"Mr. Basingstoke," she said, quite untruly, "doesn't care much about motoring."

"Mr.—? Oh, your brother! Well, we did very well without him before, didn't we? Do you re-

KENILWORTH

member what a jolly drive we had, and a jolly lunch; in point of fact, practically everything was jolly until *he* turned up. I wished him far enough, I can tell you, and I hope you did. Say you did."

"Of course I didn't," she had to say.

"Well, he'd no right to be stuffy if another fellow took care of you when he couldn't be bothered to."

"You know it wasn't that. You know it was a mistake."

"I know a good deal," he said, "more than you think for." And he smiled, trying to meet her eyes.

"It's cold here," she found herself saying. "I was just going up. I don't like dungeons. Do you?"

"I like this one," said he. "Anywhere where *you* are, don't you know—a palace and all that—"

"I really must go," she said. "My brother won't know where I am."

"No," he said, with meaning, "he won't." And he set his two hands to the pillars of the arch under which he stood and swayed to and fro, looking at her.

"I must really go. Will you let me pass, Mr. Schultz, please."

"Not till you tell me to send for my car. I've set my heart on those drives with you. Our

THE INCREDIBLE HONEYMOON

brother can stay behind if he doesn't care for motoring. *I* don't want him, and I'll take care *you* don't miss him."

"Do, please," she said, "let me pass."

"No," said he. "I've got you and I mean to keep you. Your brother—"

"He's not my brother," she said, on a sudden resolution. "We told you that because, because—"

"Don't bother to explain," he said, smiling. That smile, in the days when that dungeon *was* a dungeon, might have cost him his life if the lady before him had had a knife and the skill to use it. Even now it was to cost him something.

"He's not my brother—we're married," she said. And at that he laughed.

"I know, my dear girl," he said. "I know all about it. But marriages like that don't last forever, and they don't prevent another gentleman playing for his own hand. I was there when he wasn't, and you let me help you."

"I wish I hadn't," said she. "I wish I'd walked all the way to London first. I didn't think—"

"You didn't think I'd got the sense to put two and two together," said he; "but I have. Come, look here. I liked your looks from the first. I thought— Never mind about that, though. I was wrong. But even now I like you better

KENILWORTH

than any girl I've ever come across. Now, look here—"

"Don't say any more," she urged, almost wildly. "Don't! I am married. You don't believe me, but I am. You were kind once; be kind now and let me go—"

It was like a prisoner imploring a jailer.

"Let you go?" he echoed. "I know better. Not till you say, 'Send for the motor,' and that you'll go out in it with me. Say that and you're free as air."

And she might have said it, for the terror that lurked in that tower was coming back, in a new dress, but the same terror. But he went on, "Come, say it, and seal the bargain prettily."

And then she said, "If you don't let me pass I swear I'll—"

What the threat would have been she hardly knew, and he never knew, for he took a step toward her with his hands outstretched, and words seemed at once to become weak and silly. She clutched her rosy sunshade at about half its length and struck full at his head. The sunshade broke. He put his hands to his temples and held them a moment.

"Now, by God," he said, "after that—" and came toward her.

And even as he moved the feet of the deliverer

THE INCREDIBLE HONEYMOON

sounded on the stairs. Hurried feet, spurning the stones, feet swifter than a man's, lighter than a woman's—little feet that gave out a thin, quick sound not like the sound of human footsteps. She called aloud on the name of the deliverer and he came, swift as the arrow from the bow of a master-archer.

"Charles!" she cried. "Charles, seize him! Hold him!"

And Charles, coming headlong into that dark place like a shaft of live white light, seized him, and held, by the leg.

Mr. Schultz did his best to defend himself, but he had no stick, and no blows of the human fist confused or troubled that white bullet head, no curses affected it, and against those white teeth no kicks or struggles availed.

"Hold him! hold him!" she cried, the joy of vicarious battle lighting her eyes.

"Confound it!" said Schultz. "Call the devil off."

"I will," said she, "from the top of the stairs. And I'll leave you this for comfort: If you behave yourself for the future I won't tell my husband about this. He'd half kill you."

"I don't know about that," said Schultz, even with Charles's teeth quietly but persistently boring his leg. "I don't know so much about that."

KENILWORTH

"I do," she said, with almost the conviction of the woman in love. "You'd better stay here till we've gone away. I'm not ungrateful for what you did for me on that day, and if you never dare to speak to me again I'll never tell."

"I don't care what you tell," said Schultz. "Call the devil off, I say."

She ran up the stairs, and at the top called out, "Charles, drop it. Come here, sir."

And Charles dropped it and came.

It was then for the first time that she felt that she was Charles's mistress, even as Edward was Charles's master.

The dog and the woman went out together into the sunshine, and there, between blue sky and green grass, embraced with all the emotions proper to deliverer and delivered. When Edward rejoined them, five minutes later, she was able to say, quite calmly:

"Yes, he found me out. He *is* clever. He is a darling."

"He deserves a jolly good hiding," said Edward, "and I've a jolly good mind to give it to him."

"Let him off this time," she said, "it was so clever of him to find me out. He hadn't hurt any of the sheep, had he?"

"No," said he, "but he might have."

"Oh, if we come to might-have-beens," said she, "I might not be here, he might not be here. We all might not be here. Think of that. No, don't look at him with that 'wait-till-I-get-you-home' expression. Forgive him and be done with it."

And when she looked at him like that, as he told himself, what could he do but forgive the dog?

"Why," he said, "of course I'll forgive him!" adding, with one of those diabolical flashes of insight to which our subconscious selves are sometimes liable. "Why, I'd forgive Schultz himself if you asked me like that."

"It isn't Mr. Schultz I want you to forgive," she said, "it's Charles—Charles that I love."

"Not Schultz whom you like."

"I hate Schultz," said she, so vehemently that he wondered. Because always before she had defended the man and called him kind and helpful. It was, however, so pleasant to him that she should hate Schultz that he put his wonder by to taste that pleasure.

She had the self-control to wait till they were gliding through the streets of Warwick before she said, "Do you want to stay here any longer?"

"Not if you don't," said he.

"I should like to go to Chester," she said, "now—this evening. Would you mind? There's such lots to see, and something might happen at any moment to stop our—"

"Our incredible honeymoon?" he said. "But what could?"

"Oh, Aunt Alice might be ill and want me"—and hated herself for the words. The moment she had uttered them she felt that in using her as a defense she had almost as good as called down the wrath of the gods on Aunt Alice, whom she loved. "Oh, a thousand things might happen," she added, quickly.

"My lady's will is my law," said Edward, and within an hour or two they were on the way to Chester. Charles did not, this time, make his journey in the dog-box. She smiled on the guard, and Charles traveled in a first-class carriage with his master and his mistress. He sat between them and was happy as only they can be happy who have combined duty and pleasure. He had chased sheep—this was obviously not wrong, since master had not punished him for it. He had bitten a stranger at mistress's bidding. Mistress was evidently one who sympathized with the natural aspirations of right-minded dogs. Charles knew now how much he loved her. He leaned himself against her, heavily asleep, now and then growling softly as he slept. His mistress felt that in his dreams he was still biting Mr. Schultz. He was.

XVI

CAERNARVON

SOMEHOW or other Chester failed to charm. Neither of them could understand why. Perhaps the Stratford Hotel had given them a momentary surfeit of half-timber; perhaps the fact that the skies turned gray and substituted drizzle for sunshine had something to do with it; perhaps it was the extreme badness of the hotel to which ill-luck led them, a hotel that smelt of stale seed-cake and bad coffee and bad mutton-fat, and was furnished almost entirely with bentwood chairs and wicker tables; perhaps it was the added aggravation of seeing a river which might have been to them a second Medway, and seeing it quite impossible and miserably pitted with little rain-spots. Whatever the reason, even next morning's sunshine and the beauty of the old walls and the old walks failed to dispel the gloom. They bought rain-coats and umbrellas in a shop that had known ruffs and farthingales, paid their hotel bill, which

CAERNARVON

was as large as the hotel was bad, and took the afternoon train to Caernarvon.

The glimpse of Conway Castle from the train cheered them a little. The sight of the sea did more—but still he felt a cloud between them, and still she felt more and more that he was aware of it. Charles sat between them, as before, and over that stout white back his eyes met hers.

"What is it?" he asked, suddenly. "Yesterday I thought it was the half-timber and the rain—this morning I thought it was yesterday, but it isn't. Something's happened that you haven't told me."

She turned her eyes from his and stroked the flappy white ears of Charles.

"Hasn't it?" he urged. "Ah, you will tell me, won't you? Was it something from the aunts?"

For there had been letters that morning, sent on from Warwick.

"No, the letters were all right. Everybody's furious except Aunt Alice, but she's the only one that matters."

"Then what is it?"

"It's almost gone," she said. "Oh, look at the rocks and the heather on that great hill."

"Then there was something," he said; "something you won't tell me."

"Not won't," she said, gently.

"Can't? Something that's happened and you can't tell me?"

He remembered how on the last night at Warwick he had held that hand of hers against his face. They had seemed so very near then. And now there was a gulf suddenly opened between them—the impassable gulf of a secret—a secret that was hers and not his.

"Yes, something did happen and I have promised not to tell you. If ever I can, I will."

"Something has come between us and you have promised not to tell me what it is?"

"Oh no—no!" she said, very earnestly, and her dear eyes looked full in his. "Nothing has come between us—nothing could—"

He realized, with some impatience, that Charles, at least, was between them. But for Charles he could, quite naturally and *ayant l'air de rien* have leaned a little toward her as he spoke—so that his shoulder might, perhaps, if she had leaned also, have just touched hers. But across Charles this could not be. And to lean, after the removal of Charles, would bear an air of premeditation not to be contemplated for an instant.

"If it's nothing that comes between us—" he said. "But even then, it's something that's made you sad, made you different. I suppose, though, it's unreasonable to expect that there shall be no

CAERNARVON

secrets between any two human beings, no matter how—how friendly they are," he ended, with conscious lameness.

"Of course it's unreasonable," she said; "it would mean, wouldn't it, that neither of us could ever be trusted by any one else? Whereas now people can tell you things they wouldn't want to tell me, and tell me things they wouldn't care about telling you."

"Then this—I'm not worrying you to tell me—but if it is somebody else's secret——"

"Well, it is," she said. "Now, are you satisfied? And if you'll only let me look at the sea and the mountains and the heather the Chester cloud will go right away. It's nearly gone now. And I've never seen any real mountains before, not mountains like these, with warm colors and soft shapes —only the Pyrenees and the Maritime Alps, and they look just like white cardboard cut into points and pasted on blue sugar-paper—that's the sky."

"It's prettier at sunrise, with the mountains like pink and white sugar, and Corsica showing like a little cloud over the sea. We had a villa at Antibes when I was a little chap, before we lost our money. We'll go there again some day, shall we, and see if the mountains have changed at all? Not this winter, I think. I've never had

THE INCREDIBLE HONEYMOON

an English winter free from work I didn't like. I must have just this one. You don't mind?"

What he hoped she wouldn't mind was less the English winter than his calm assumption that there was plenty of time, that they would always be together and might go where they would and when—since all the future was before them—all the future, and each other's companionship all through it.

"Why should I mind?" she answered. "I've never had a free winter in England, either, or anywhere else, for that matter."

"Then that's settled," said he, comfortably, "and you can't think what a comfort it is to me that you don't hate Charles. You might so easily have hated dogs."

"If I'd been that sort of person I shouldn't be here."

"Ah, but Charles might so easily have been the one kind of dog you couldn't stand. He's not everybody's dog, by any means. Are you, Charles? Of course it's almost incredible that this earth should contain people who don't like Charles, yet so it is."

"The people he's bitten?"

"Oh, those!" said Edward, adding, with a fine air of tolerance, "I could almost find excuses for them—they've not seen the finer aspects of his character. No, there are actually human beings to

CAERNARVON

whom Charles's personality does not appeal—persons whom he has borne with patiently, whom he has refrained from biting, or even sniffing at the trousers legs of. Prejudice is a mysterious and terrible thing. Oh, but it's a good world—all the same."

"Isn't it," she said, "with the sun shining and the mountains and the rocks and the sea all there, just like a picture? Oh, there's no doubt but it's a beautiful world."

"And you and I and Charles going out to see it all together. It's a fine world, every bit of it—and the little bit we're just coming to is Caernarvon."

Caernarvon it was, and they spent nearly a week there. The castle is all that a castle should be; and as for the sea, what can be better, unless it's in Cornwall; and there is Anglesea, lying flat against the sky, and the Elephant Mountain and the Seven Sisters, and old Snowdon topping all.

The inn was comfortable, the weather had grown kind again, the hostler was one of those to whom Charles's personality so much appealed that the dog was almost too replete with good living to appreciate the rats provided for his recreation. This hostler, Owen Llewellyn, became such an enthusiast in the service of Charles that Mr. Basingstoke was only able by a fortunate chance, the strong exercise of authority, and a golden offering for the soothing of wounded feelings to stop the entertainment which Owen had arranged with several of his friends in a handy field and the cool of the evening: a quiet little dog-fight, as the friends indignantly explained, with Charles and a worthy antagonist filling the leading rôles.

"It isn't as if the dogs wouldn't enjoy it more than any one else, and me putting all my money on your dog, sir," one of the friends (from London) complained. "There ain't nothing that that there dog 'u'd love better nor a bit of a scrap. An' you to go agin the animal's natural desires and keep him for a lap-dog for the lady. It ain't right," he ended, feelingly, as the lap-dog was led off, yapping defiance at the adversary whom, so his admirers swore, he could have licked hollow with one paw tied behind him.

It was at Caernarvon that Edward and his princess lived the quiet life that does not lead to sight-seeing. There was something poignantly domestic to his mind in those long mornings in green fields or among the broken and still beautiful colonnades of the castle, he with a book from which he read to her, she with some work of embroidery in which a bright needle flashed among pleasant-colored silks. It was in the castle, in one of those mysterious narrow passages, that they came face to face with a tall, handsome man of middle age, who shook Edward's hand with extreme vigor, clapped him on the back, and announced that he would have run a mile for the sake of seeing him. Edward would have run two to avoid the meeting, because the eyes of the back-clapper were turned on Katherine, awaiting the introduction which must come. Colonel Bertram, an old friend of Edward's father's, knew well enough that Edward was an only child. No brother-and-sister tale was possible here.

"Do you hang out in these parts?" Edward asked. "I wonder you knew me. I don't believe we've met since I was about sixteen."

While he spoke he looked a question at her, and read the slightest possible sign with which she answered.

"Colonel Bertram—my wife. Katherine, the Colonel used to tip me sovereigns when I was at school, and he gave me my first pony."

The colonel's grip ground her rings into her hand. "'Pon my word!" he said, "I don't know when I've been so pleased. You must come and dine with us, my boy, to-night— To-morrow? Make him come, Mrs. Basingstoke. I know it's not manners to intrude on a honeymoon, but I am such an old friend, and our meeting like this is such a remarkable coincidence, almost like the finger of Providence—upon my soul it is."

"It's very, very nice of you to ask us," she said, in a voice of honey, "but, unfortunately, we're leaving this afternoon."

"Well, at any rate, let's lunch together. No, of course; too late for that. Well, look here, you've seen the castle, of course; come and see over the prison. I'm governor there, for my sins. Come and let me show you my prison!"

His simple pride in the only sight he had to show prevailed even against the shrinking she felt and did not wholly understand.

"When are you leaving? The six o'clock train? Plenty of time. We've made wonderful reforms, I can tell you. The cells are pictures, perfect pictures. 'Pon my word, I never was so glad to see any one. And so you're married. Dear, dear, dear! Makes me feel an old boy, that it does! The young ones growing up around us—eh, what?"

He led the way out of the castle, and Edward and Katherine exchanged behind his cordial back glances almost of despair. They had not wanted to leave Caernarvon, but Edward could only bless Katherine for her decision. The relations of Mr. and Mrs. Basingstoke could never have stood the affectionate cross-questionings of Mrs. Bertram. They must go; Katherine was right.

CAERNARVON

Katherine, meantime, was wishing she had invented a headache, an appointment at the local dentist's, had even simulated a swoon at Colonel Bertram's feet, before she had consented to visit a prison.

From the first moment of her entrance there the prison appalled her. It was a very nice prison, as prisons go. But the grating at the door, the locks that clicked, the polished keys, the polished handcuffs, the prison records which their host exhibited with so much ingenuous enthusiasm; the cells, one little cage after another in which human birds were pent. . . .

"What have they all done?" she asked, as they walked along a stone-paved gallery; and wished she had not asked, for the details of horrible crimes were the last things she wished to hear.

"Oh, petty felonies, mostly," said the governor, airily.

It seemed more and more horrible to her that she and he and the governor should tread the mazes of this place free to come and go as they chose, while these other human beings, for whatever fault—and it seemed the faults could hardly rank as crimes—should be here encaged, never more to go out free till their penance should have purged them.

"I suppose one mustn't give them anything?"

THE INCREDIBLE HONEYMOON

"A little good advice wouldn't be amiss. 'Don't do it any more,' and so on. Would you like to give them an address, Mrs. Basingstoke?"

She hated his badinage. "I mean tobacco or chocolate or books, or anything that they'd *like*," she explained, patiently.

"No, no," said the governor. "They aren't pets, you know. Mustn't feed them through the bars as though they were rabbits or guinea-pigs. The townspeople *will* throw tobacco over into the yard. Can't stop them. But of course we punish the offenders very severely whenever we manage to bring it home to them."

The horrible sense of slavery grew on her—the prisoners were slaves to the warders, the warders slaves, and super-subservient slaves, to the governor, the governor himself a slave to some power unseen but all-potent.

She watched her opportunity and while Colonel Bertram was explaining to Edward the method of the manufacture of post-office bags she opened her purse in her pocket and let all its contents fall loose therein. Then she gathered the money in a handful, careful that no rattle or chink should betray her, and when the governor was explaining how wire netting, spread over each gallery to catch any object thrown from above rendered suicide difficult, if not impossible, she knotted the money in her handkerchief. Then she watched for further opportunity, hoping against hope, for it seemed that her chance would never come. There were eyes everywhere.

"If I can't do it here, I'll buy tobacco and throw it over the wall," she told herself.

It was in the kitchen that the chance came. Three prisoners were there acting as cooks, and the governor had sent the attendant warder on some errand, to order tea for them in his office, as events showed.

"Very nice—very neat—very clean." She praised all in the simplest and most direct words.

The governor again addressed himself to Edward. It was a tale of poaching that he told—the theft of two hares and a pheasant—a desperate crime duly punished. He and Edward left the kitchen, talking. She followed, but first she laid her hand on a table near the door and looked full at the nearest prisoner. Then she smiled. The three smiled back at her. Then she opened her hand, showing plainly the knotted handkerchief. "Good luck!" she said, low, but so that they all heard her.

Then she followed the governor and Edward, but at the door she turned and kissed her hand to the three prisoners. The faces they turned to her will stay with her as long as she lives. Wonder,

THE INCREDIBLE HONEYMOON

delight, incredulity—that any one—that *she* should have cared to say "good luck," should have smiled at them, should have left them her handkerchief, though they did not yet know what was in it. The wonder and worship in their eyes brought tears to her own.

They were still there when the governor turned.

"A cup of tea, now, Mrs. Basingstoke," he said, "it's all ready."

She answered hurriedly, "It's very kind of you, but, do you know, if you don't mind, I think we ought to be going. We've got to pack and all that."

Colonel Bertram, who was no fool, heard the quivering voice and saw the swimming eyes. "So sorry," he said, "but charmed to have met you—charmed," and stood back for her to pass the door of the corridor. "*I* understand," he said; "your wife's a bit upset. Ladies often are; they don't understand the law, you know, the great principles of property and the law. Don't mention it; I like them soft-hearted. You're a fortunate man, my boy—deuced fortunate. Good-by. So very, very pleased we happened to meet. Good-by."

The well-oiled locks clicked to let them out. In the street she caught his arm and clung to it.

"There, there!" he spoke as one speaks to a

CAERNARVON

frightened child. "It's all over; don't distress yourself."

"It's not all over for them," she said.

"Prisons have to be," said Edward.

"Have they?" said she. "I suppose they do, but such little things. To take a pair of boots because your feet are cold and you have no money, and to pay for what you've done—with *that*. Horrible! horrible!"

Neither of them spoke again till they were nearly at the hotel. Then he said, "What did you give them?"

"What do you mean?"

"I saw you knotting something in that little scented handkerchief of yours. What was it you gave them."

"Every penny I had. And I said, 'Good luck to you,' and I kissed my hand to them. There!" she said, defiantly.

"It was like you," he said, and took her arm. "But I wish I hadn't let you go inside the place. I didn't realize how it would be to you. I didn't realize what it would be to me."

"It was silly of me, I suppose," she said.

"I dare say. But you were lucky; I only managed to drop my tobacco-pouch among the post-office bags, but our guilt is equal. The sooner we get out of Caernarvon the better. By the way, don't let's catch the six-o'clock train to nowhere in particular. Let's take a carriage and drive to Llanberis and see the slate-quarries and go up Snowdon."

"Don't let's ever go into another prison," she said, blinking so that the tears should drop off her eyelashes and not run down her face, "it hurts so horribly, and we can't do any good."

"Not do any good?" he said. "Do you suppose that life can ever be the same to a man to whom you've smiled and kissed your hand? Ah, I don't mean it for empty gallantry, my dear. I mean that to know that you, free and beautiful, care for them in their misery and imprisonment—don't you think that's worth something?"

"If it is, I'm glad we went," said she.

Their departure for Llanberis, though sudden, was the less deplored by the hotel management because of a regrettable misunderstanding which had arisen during the afternoon between Charles and the house cat.

XVII

LLANBERIS

LLANBERIS, prim and small, and very, very Welsh, lies in the shadow of great Snowdon, and all about it the lesser and more gracious mountains—the mountains of green and purple and brown—stand with their heads against the sky, bathing their feet in great lakes of smooth, brown water. The inn has a beautiful and terraced garden; the stream from the waterfall under Snowdon runs tumbling and gurgling down its rocky bed. "The peace that is upon the lonely hills" may be yours at the cost of a little breathless, happy climbing; the deeper peace of valleys and lake may be yours for no more trouble than it takes to walk a couple of hundred yards from the door of your inn. That the hotel was full did not seem to matter—the other guests were off early, in breaks and wagonettes, spending the long days in excursions from which they returned late and hilarious, breaking the soft night quiet with loud laughter and snatches of the kind of songs that nowadays delight the great heart of the people. Trippers from Manchester and Liverpool came for the day, but never strayed far from the inn, or, if they did, went up Snowdon by the tiny railway. Everywhere, save on the way that led to Snowdon, you were sure of quiet or peace, of a world where two could be alone together.

Here the two tried to take up again the life of ordered ease that had been theirs at Caernarvon, the little life they had prized and cherished till the governor of Caernarvon prison had thrown a stone into their magic pool, shattering all its mirrored beauty. They spent long mornings on the hillside, cushioned by the heather; long evenings by the lakeside, always careful to choose their resting-place so that they need not see the scars where the waste slate is tipped into the lake, slowly overlaying the green and graceful margin with which Nature, if you let her alone, frames all water mirrors. And once they went as far as the mysterious Round Tower, which stands alone, with no entrance but the doorway high above your head.

"What a place to keep your enemy in," he said, "or your friend! Suppose the tower had been my stronghold, in the old days. I could have brought my princess here, and snapped my fingers at her relations drawn round the tower in a ring, shaking their fists at me from their coal-black steeds, and vowing vengeance when the tower should yield—which, of course, it never would."

"Your princess would have starved," she said, "and you with her."

"Not at all," he assured her; "you underrate the resources of round towers. To say nothing of the goats and sheep which we should drive in and lower to the basement when our scout brought news that your kinsmen were sending out the fiery cross or the blood eagle, or whatever it was that they did send out; and there's an inexhaustible well inside the tower, and of course we should have sacks of meal and casks of mead."

"But the enemy—her relations, I mean—would have all the sheep on the mountains and all the flour in the mills. You'd have to give in, in the end."

"You forget the underground passage. When we were tired of mocking your uncles and cousins through the arrow-slits of our tower we'd quietly creep away to our great castle—it's at Caernarvon, you know—and call together all my uncles and cousins and sally out and have a great battle, and the sound of our blows on their helmets would be heard on the far side of Anglesea, and down to the very southernmost marches of Merioneth."

THE INCREDIBLE HONEYMOON

"But suppose her relations won the battle and shut you up in a dungeon and put her into a convent?"

"Oh, they wouldn't. All our armor would be so perfectly tempered that nobody would be hurt. It would be like a tournament, and at the end, just as your senior uncle and I had unhorsed each other and were about to perish, mutually cloven to the chine, you would rush between us—in white, with your hair flowing like a thunder-cloud behind you—and say to each of us, 'Spare him for my sake.' And of course we should. And then there would be a banquet in the great hall at Caernarvon and clean rushes on the floor, and you and I and all our relations sitting in state on the dais, and you'd be wearing your gown of cloth of gold and your cloak of vair, and all your jewels—and I should have my furred gown and my great ring, and we should drink out of the big silver drinking-bowl—mead and strong ale—and feast our guests and their men-at-arms and all our own people on roast boars' heads and barons of beef, and all live happily ever afterward."

"I don't think she'd wear her ermine mantle. Wouldn't she wear the one of woven red, with your coat of arms embroidered on it, and the gold beads you brought her from the East when you went to the wars there?"

LLANBERIS

"Perhaps you would," he conceded. "I believe I could climb up to that doorway. I should like to—just to be sure there's really a well inside."

"No, don't," said she, "because you might find out that there wasn't; or that this isn't really the tower that has the underground passage leading to Caernarvon, and then we should know that we're not really remembering that other life when you carried her off, but only making it up."

"Of course we remember it. Do you remember whether you were angry with me for carrying you off."

"If she hadn't wanted to be carried off," she said, demurely, "she wouldn't have been. Or if she hadn't been able to help herself she'd have found a little knife, like the brown bride, or else something to put in your mead-cup, so that the first draught you had from her hand would have been the last. She wasn't the sort of woman to be taken against her will. Come away before you spoil the story with any more questions. I liked it best when we took the tale for granted—"

It was high up among the heather, with Charles safely tethered and the steep hillside dotted with hundreds and hundreds of sheep, that the talk grew earnest and dwelt not on dreams of old days, but the desire of new ones.

"Do you remember," he said, "what you told

THE INCREDIBLE HONEYMOON

me when we were going to Warwick?" He spoke as though this had been a long time ago, as, indeed, by any count but time it was. "You remember about the scattered farms, and the way the little houses call to you to come home."

"Yes," she said.

"All that you said about the life—it was like my other self speaking."

"You mean that when I spoke, your inside self said, 'Yes, yes; that's what I mean'?"

"I mean more than that. My inside self said, 'Yes, yes, that's what I always meant. That's what I meant and what I wanted before ever I met you.' Then meeting you obscured everything else, but when you spoke I saw that what I had always wanted rhymed with what you had always wanted. But I want to be quite sure. May I ask questions?"

"Yes."

"Suppose we had been really married—would you have been contented to spend your working life on a farm, to live just that life that you spoke of that day going to Warwick?"

She did not speak for a moment, and for a moment he wished that he had not questioned. And when she did speak it was not to give him an answer.

"I didn't believe it was possible," she said. "I

thought people couldn't make farming succeed, nowadays, and I don't think I could bear to spend my working life, as you call it, on a thing that is foredoomed to failure."

"Nor could I; and I don't mean to, either. My farm will succeed. If it costs me every penny I have it shall succeed. I shall go a new way to work. You know I've really got quite a lot of money, and I have a plan."

"Tell me about it."

"It's quite simple, and absolutely opposed to all the accursed teachings of political economy. Of course I shall get the best machinery and the best seeds and the best implements. But I shall also get the best labor."

"Doesn't every one try to do that?"

"Oh yes, every farmer tries to get the best labor he can, at current rates. I sha'n't bother about the current rates. I shall get the best men that are to be got and I shall pay them wages that will make them glad to come to me rather than to any one else. If I find a man's good I shall give him a share in the profits of the farm; if I find he isn't any good I shall sack him."

"I wonder," she said, "whether you'd have the heart to sack any one?"

"I might hesitate to sack a mere fool," he admitted. "I might be tempted to keep him on and find some work for him that even a fool could do. But I'd chuck a slacker at a week's notice and never turn a hair. You'll see; I shall have failures, many of them, but the whole thing won't be a failure. Before I've done I shall have the best carters, the best dairy-women, the best bailiff, and the best plowman and the most successful farm in the country. You don't know how men can work who are working for themselves and not just for a master."

"You mean to make it a sort of communal farm?"

"Never," he said. "That's the last thing I mean it to be. But it will be a profit-sharing farm, and I shall run it. It's my own idea, the darling of my soul, and I won't trust its life to any other man. I'm almost afraid to trust it to you, for fear you should not be kind to it. But if what you said on the way to Warwick meant something that lasts in you—not just the beautiful thoughts of the moment—tell me, if we were really married could you endure a life like that?"

"I should know nothing about it; I should be of no use. And we're not married—"

"You could learn; we could both learn. Let's pretend for a moment that we're really going to spend our lives together, anyhow. Let's leave

Mrs. Basingstoke out of it. Would Miss Basingstoke have been able to endure such a life?"

"Miss Basingstoke would have loved it," she said. "Miss Basingstoke would have done her best to learn, and—she isn't really stupid, you know—I think Miss Basingstoke would have succeeded."

"It would need patience," he said, "patience and bravery and loving-kindness and gentleness and firmness and unselfishness."

"And curiosity," she said. "That quality, at least, Miss Basingstoke has. She would have wanted to know all about everything, and that's one way of learning. She wants, now, to know ever so much more. Tell her everything that you've thought of about it, everything you've decided or not decided."

"You'll be kind to my darling dream, then," he said. "Well, here goes."

And with that he told her, and she listened and questioned, and he answered again till the shadows had grown heavy in the valley and they were very late indeed for dinner.

You cannot be long in Llanberis without wanting to "see over" a slate-quarry. It was on their fifth day that the desire came to these two. The mention of Colonel Bertram's name gained for them a personally conducted tour through the rows of little slate-roofed sheds where skilled workmen strip and chip and shape the flakes of quarried slate till they are the size and form needed for roofing cottages and schools and Nonconformist chapels. Having seen how the slate is treated in the sheds, they were taken into the quarry itself to see how the slate is got.

A big slate-quarry is a very impressive sight. You walk across a great amphitheater whose walls of slate rise high above you, their green-trimmed edges sharply cut against the sky. You pick your way among pools of water so smooth, so clear, that they reflect like mirrors the blue sky and the high slate walls of the quarry. One such pool—the largest—lay in the middle of the vast amphitheater, and in it the towering cliffs of slate were reflected even more clearly than in the others.

"I never saw such reflections," she was saying, as they skirted the big pond. "They're almost more real than the real thing. I am glad we came here; it's all so clear and bright and new-looking. I wonder—"

"I wouldn't walk quite so near the edge, if I was you, sir," said the foreman, who was their guide.

"Why?" Edward asked, gazing at the reflection of high cliffs in the pool at his side, "is the water deep—"

LLANBERIS

And even as he spoke his eyes were opened; but before he could obey their mandate, with a cry that went to his heart and held it she caught his arm and pulled him back. For in that instant she, too, had seen that this pool which reflected so perfectly the tall precipices of the quarry was not a pool at all, but another deep quarry within the first, and that what it held was no reflection, but a sheer and dreadful depth of precipice going down—she would not look to see how far. And he had been walking within six inches of its brink, carelessly and at ease, as one does walk by the safely shelving edge of any pond.

She did not let his arm go when she had drawn him away from that perilous edge; she held it closely pressed against her side, and when he looked at her he saw that her face was white and changed. The great precipice above them swayed a little to her eyes—she dared not look at the precipice below. She held his arm closely and more closely, folding both hands on it. The foreman was saying something. Neither of them heard what it was, only both caught the concluding words:

"Perhaps you'd like to see the place, sir."

"Thank you," said Edward, mechanically, "and then I think we must leave you. It's been most kind of you to show us all this; we've been most interested."

THE INCREDIBLE HONEYMOON

Her heart was beating in so wild an ecstasy of thanksgiving for an unspeakable horror escaped, his heart was beating in so passionate and proud and humble a recognition of what her touch on his arm confessed, that neither of them heard the foreman's words or guessed at the meaning of what he was calmly and coldly telling them. Only afterward the memory of his words came back, bringing with it understanding. They were led across a flat wilderness of splintered slate toward the tall cliff from which now and then came the noise like thunder which blasting-powder makes when it does its work. They two, hardly conscious of anything but that they held each other—the one who had been in danger, safe; the other passionately grateful for that other's safety; and the endangered one, passionately sensible of her passionate gratitude, heard not a word that the foreman spoke, though he spoke all the time.

"You are here; I hold you safe; but, oh, if I had lost you!" her heart was singing to a breathless, syncopated measure.

"You cared; you cared as much as this. If I had fallen over that perilous edge . . . Oh, but you care, you care! It is as much as this to you," his heart sang, keeping time to hers.

It was a trance of mutual meeting emotion such as they had not yet known. In that one mo-

LLANBERIS

ment, when he walked the narrow edge of that precipice and when she had seen the precipice for the horror it was, she learned more than in all her life before. And he, in the moments that followed, knew, beyond possibility of mistake or misunderstanding, what it was that she had learned. If only they could have walked straight out of that quarry into the world of stream and mountain, the world where you are only two—but the foreman was there, walking and talking, and at last stopping and saying:

"This is where it happened."

And they came out of their dream to find themselves close to the slate cliff at whose base lay great blocks of slate newly fallen, and to see the flat slate flakes at their feet, brown and wet.

"Where what happened?" Edward asked, vaguely.

"What I've been telling you about," said the foreman, aggrieved. "Where one of our workmen was killed just now, blasting; that's his blood what you're standing in," said he.

Then, indeed, she clung to his arm. "Take me away," she whispered. "Oh, why does everything turn horrible like this? It's like a horrible dream. Let's get away. Give him something and let's get away."

"It's not my fault," said the foreman, in very

injured tones. "She said she'd like to see it. I wondered, at the time, but there's no accounting for females, is there?"

They got away from the place—out of the quarry and into the road. They found the stream that flows from the waterfall under Snowdon, and the flagged path that lies beside the stream. They passed along it, she still clinging to his arm. Presently a smooth, mossy rock invited them, and before either of them knew it they were seated there, side by side, and she was weeping on his shoulder.

He did not need her whispered words that broke a long silence—"Thank God, you're safe"—to tell him what he had to think, nor what, from that hour, he had to live for.

"But, oh," she said at last, lifting her face from his coat-sleeve, "what a horrible day! We've struck a streak of horrible things. Let's go back to the south, where things aren't like this."

"We'll go to-night, if you like," he said.

"Yes," she answered, eagerly, "yes. But this isn't the end. I feel there's something more coming—I felt it at Chester. It wasn't only that thing I couldn't tell you—something's going to happen to separate us."

"Nothing can—but you," he said, hugging to his heart all that her admission implied.

LLANBERIS

"I feel that something will," she said.

And he, for all that he laughed at her fears and her predictions, with pride and joy swelling in his heart till they almost broke the resolution of quiescence, of waiting, of submitting his will to her will, yet felt in those deep caves that lie behind the heart, behind the soul, behind the mind of man, the winds of coming misfortune blow chilly.

It was no surprise to either of them to find at the hotel a telegram for Mrs. Basingstoke:

> Aunt Alice much worse. Please come at once.

It was signed with the name of the aunt whose dog-cart had run over Charles, and beneath whose legs Charles had experienced his miraculous resurrection from death.

There was no reason to mistrust this telegram as they had mistrusted the advertisement. But she said to herself, "There! That's because of what I said at Warwick."

They caught the last train to London that night, and through the long, lamp-lit journey Charles no longer lay between them. The white, bullet head lay on her lap—but on her other side was Edward, and her shoulder and his touched all the way, even as, on the journey to Warwick, he had dreamed of their touching. They spoke little; it seemed as though everything had been

THE INCREDIBLE HONEYMOON

said. Only when her head drooped against his shoulder and he knew that she had fallen asleep he felt no sense of daring, no doubts as to his rights or her resentments when he passed his arm around her and rested his chin on her soft hair, gazing straight before him in the flickering half-light while she slept—oh, dreams come true—upon his breast.

XVIII

LONDON

IT was very late when they parted on the doorstep of the house in Hyde Park Square.

"I don't know how to let you go," he said, and took both her hands, regardless of the cabman's stony attention. "I shall just go back to my rooms in Montague Street—Thirty-seven; I've written it down for you. And, look here, I won't come and see you and I won't bother you, but if you want me I'll be there. You must just do what you want to do."

What she wanted to do was to jump into the waiting taxicab and go back with him into that world of fine and delicate adventure where were blue skies, gold sun, green leaves, the mystery of mountains, the sparkle of water, and the velvet of old lawns; and, for each in the soul of the other, a whole world of unexplored wonder and delight.

What she said was: "Thank you. I will write and tell you what happens. Good-by—oh, good-

THE INCREDIBLE HONEYMOON

by. I feel as though I ought to ask you to forgive me."

"For what?"

"Oh, I don't know," she said, "but—no—I don't know; but you do understand that I couldn't stay away when she asked for me. She's the only person in the world, except you, that I — that ever— Good-by!"

There was a moment of hesitation which, later, in the recollection of it, thrilled them both. Then the cabman had the satisfaction, such as it was, of seeing one of his fares raise to his lips the fingers of the other. Then the knocker sounded softly, the heavy door opened and received her into a warmly lamp-lit hall, closed again, and left him alone.

When he reached Montague Street rain was falling and a chill wind blew. He had not been expected and his rooms were dusty and disheveled. Intensely quiet, too; through the roar of London far below one could almost hear the silence of these deserted rooms where, day by day, while he had been out in the beautiful bright world, the dim dust had slowly settled down.

It was characteristic of him that he lit a big fire and carried his bedding out and spread it in the growing glow and warmth. "I'm not going to risk a cold in the head at this crisis of my affairs," he told himself, "even if she doesn't care—and Heaven knows how she can! I needn't make myself a ridiculous and disgusting object in her eyes."

To the same end he set the kettle on the fire and made hot coffee for himself. When, at last, he turned into well-aired sheets he found that he could not sleep.

"Confound the coffee!" he said, and tried to attribute to that brown exotic elixir the desperate sense of futility and emptiness which possessed him. His mind assured him that there was nothing the matter with him but coffee; but his heart said: "You won't see her in the morning. You won't spend the day with her to-morrow, nor the next day, nor the next." And his heart cursed the mock marriage and all the reservations and abstentions that it demanded. "If she had been really my wife—" If she had been really his wife he would have called three times a day to know how things were with her. He would have seen her, held her hands, felt again the confiding droop of her head on his shoulder. But as it was—She had consented to the mock marriage, he knew, because she did not desire to give him any rights, not even the right to ring at her aunt's front door and ask for Mrs. Basingstoke.

He fell asleep at last, and dreamed that they

had taken an unfurnished flat in a neolithic cave and that he had killed a bear and was dragging it home to show her. The bear seemed to be not quite dead, for it was growling, and its weight on his back awoke him, to find that Charles had thought his master's shoulders a convenient site for slumber. He sleepily had it out with Charles, and when he slept again he dreamed that he and she had decided to live in a captive balloon. She was already installed, but he could find no ladder long enough to reach her. She was laughing down at him and showering pink rose-leaves on his upturned face when he woke to find Charles conscientiously licking his ears. This time he found energy to get up and put a closed door between himself and Charles, and then he dreamed that he had arranged to meet her under the clock at Charing Cross Station, and that the Government had just decided to establish uniformity in railway stations, and had called every station Charing Cross, and had, moreover, furnished each station with six hundred and sixty-six clocks, which all ticked louder than Big Ben. He awoke, and it was morning, and there were no clocks ticking, but from beyond the door came the measured thump-thump-thump of Charles's tail on the floor of the sitting-room. So all night he had dreamed of her, yet never once seen her.

LONDON

"If I believed in omens—" he said, and rang, to make known his return to the people of the house.

While his sitting-room was being put in order he went down to Covent Garden and came back with his arms full of roses and white lilies, which he set up in mugs and pots of Grès de Flandre and old brass and green Bruges ware.

"I wish you'd only 'a' told me, sir," said his landlady, kindly but aggrieved. "I wouldn't have had you come home and find the place all of a mess like this, not for a pound, I wouldn't. But you never wrote nor nothing, and the dust it do incriminate so. But if you're going out for the day I'll make it all as clean as a whistle by this evening. It's a twelve-hour job, so it is. If I'd only known you was to be expected."

"But you didn't know," said Edward, "and it's not going to be a twelve-hour job, but a two-hour job. I'll go out for two hours, and when I come back I sha'n't know the place, shall I? You'll work like a good fairy. I know you."

"Go on with you, sir," she advised. "You will have your joke."

"I was never more serious. You see, a lady might call." He voiced in words what he had not dared to voice in his heart.

"Oh, if it's a lady," said the landlady—and

THE INCREDIBLE HONEYMOON

through the tired, ridged, gray, London face something pretty and immortally young stirred and sparkled—"*the* young lady, sir, if I might make so bold?"

"You've hit it, Mrs. Jilks," he said—"*the* lady. If she comes before I come back—but I don't think she will—beg her to wait and say I'll be back by noon. Come on, Charles."

He went and sat in Regents Park and tried to fancy himself once more in the deep peace of the Welsh Hills till Charles had a difference of opinion with a Cocker spaniel and dreams were set to flight.

He went back, hoping against hope that he might find her there. She was not there, nor did she come. Why should she? In the middle of the afternoon came a letter; it had no beginning. It said:

I had a stiff and stifling interview with my aunt—the one Charles came to life under the knees of in the cart. She was as horrid as any one could possibly be. She reproached me for marrying a pauper, and said I'd better have stuck to the piano-tuner unless you were he in disguise! I was as dumb as a mule—indeed, I almost felt my ears beginning to lie back, as mules' ears do when they've decided they aren't going to, whatever it is. Presently I got it out of her that Aunt Alice's attack is very serious. If she gets over it she's to go to Switzerland; there's an old school friend out there that she loves, and who wants frightfully to have her there.

LONDON

So then I shall be able to come back, and we'll go out together again and see the world. You won't worry about me, will you? Because this house is quite the lap of. And you know that I wouldn't have broken off our mock-wedding tour for anything in the world except for her—because . . . but you know all that. Give my love to Charles.

"Yours sincerely" was crossed out, and a postscript added:

I don't know how to end this letter. I won't end it. I'll just put something at the end to show that this isn't the end —of our times together, I mean.
(To be continued.)

He thought it the prettiest, wittiest ending in the world.

His room was neat as a new pin, as Mrs. Jilks had promised. The roses and the lilies made it what Mrs. Jilks called a perfect bower. "Any one could tell," she assured him, "that it was *the* young lady you was expecting. Why, it's like a wedding already! She's sure to come soon, sir, and I'll have the kettle on the boil and make her a nice cup of tea the minute she comes."

But she did not come, and he had the nice cup of tea alone, unless you count Charles, who ate seven large doughnuts—seven for sixpence—in seven great gulps—with no resultant modification of his natural high spirits. Another day went by, and another, and she did not come. Edward realized that she would not come, and that he had been a fool ever to half hope that she would.

He drugged the empty hours with shopping. He wandered about London buying things—the oddest things. He bought a pair of cut-crystal lusters and the skin of a leopard, a *papier-mâché* fire-screen and a string of amber beads six feet long. He sent the amber to her in a sandalwood box cunningly carved and inlaid with ivory and ebony and silver. That was on the first day. Her second letter thanked him for it:

How did you know that yellow was my fortunate color? I was born under the sign of the lion, so a fortune-teller told me, so all yellow stones are lucky for me. I am so sorry that you have to be in London in the summer. Wouldn't you like to go into the country? Auntie is a little better.

So then he went out and bought the topaz brooch that he had thought of buying when he first saw it in that jolly little shop in Vigo Street. And he sent her that with the topaz necklace he had bought in Warwick.

They are beautiful [she wrote] and I love them, but you are not to be extravagant. I should like to write you a long letter, but auntie gets restless if I'm not sitting beside her. She's really getting better, but I'm afraid it will be several weeks . . . and she keeps asking me not to leave her. I wish I could ask you to come here, to see me. There are lots of odd minutes, when she's asleep. But my other aunt would certainly be hateful to you—and I couldn't stand that.

Again and again he asked himself why he had promised, voluntarily promised, not to call at the house. What had he been thinking of? He had been thinking of her, of course; he had wanted to make things easy for her. He had at least made them very hard for himself. He missed her every hour of the day; he would not have believed that he could have missed anything so much.

The time crawled by; the hours were long and the days interminable. Even buying things—a luxury in which he allowed himself considerable latitude—could not possess the empty spaces in a life that had been filled with her presence.

And to her, moving gently in the curtained stillness of the sick-room, among the medicine-bottles and the apparatus of sickness as the rich know it, holding the thin hand that came out of a scented, soft bed to cling to hers, it seemed that either this ordered quietude was a dream, or else that nothing in the last few weeks was true, had been true, could ever be true again. The escape, the flight, the Medway days, the reckless mock marriage, the life of fine and delicate adventure, the blue sky, the green leaves, the mystery of mountains, the sparkle of water, and the velvet of old lawns, the constant and deepening comradeship of a man of whose existence a month ago she had not so much as dreamed—could these be real—all these which she had renounced to come to the sick woman who longed for her—had these really been hers—could they ever be hers again?

Suffering had broken down the consistent unselfishness of a lifetime, and the aunt clung to her as children cling, frightened in the dark. "You won't leave me," she said, over and over again. "Your husband won't mind. It won't be for long."

"Of course I'll not leave you," she said, and wondered at the thrill her aunt's words gave her and the pang she felt as she uttered her own.

Every day while the aunt slept she crept away and went out into the air—the first day into bright sunshine which was unbearable; after that into the quiet, lamp-lit dusk of the square at night. The London night was so unlike night on the Welsh Hills that it seemed a medium that could not torment her with memories. Whereas the sunshine was the same sunshine which had lain like a benediction in that far country of delight. The lilacs and snowberries in the square inclosure, which were dried and dusty by day, borrowed from the kindly twilight the air of fresh groves, and among their somber shadows she walked as in some garden of dusky enchantments, where, alone with her dreams and her memories, she could weave, out of the past and the future, a web of glory to clothe the cold walls of the empty room which, she began to perceive, life without Edward was, and must be.

It was on the third evening, as she stood, fumbling with the key of the garden, she knew that some one stood on the pavement just behind her, and, turning sharply, was face to face with Mr. Schultz.

He raised his hat and smiled at her; held out a hand, even. She was child enough to put her two hands behind her, and woman enough to hope that he hated to see her do it. She was surprised to find herself alert and alive to the interest of the encounter; not afraid at all, only interested. Gone was the panic terror which had overwhelmed her in the Kenilworth dungeon. Anger and resentment remained, but stronger than either was curiosity, so she stood with her hands behind her, looking at him.

"Oh, very well," he said; "just as you like. I want a few words with you."

"I don't want to talk to you," she said, and locked the square gate again.

"Couldn't we walk around the garden once or

twice?" he asked. "I know you don't want to talk to me, but I want to talk to you. I'm sorry if I upset you that day in the ruins, but it's nothing to the way your dog upset me. I had to have it cauterized, besides doing completely for the only decent suit I had with me. Besides, you hit me, you know, with your parasol. Come, don't bare malice. I don't. Call it quits and open the square door."

Now you may think it was quite easy for her to turn her back on Mr. Schultz and go back to her aunt's house, leaving him planted there, but it was not really easy, because she wanted something of the man, and if she turned her back with sufficient firmness it might be that she would never see him again. What she wanted was the remission of the promise she had made him, unasked and of her own initiative—the promise that she would not tell Edward of that day in the dungeon.

"I can't open the square gate for you," she said. "If you've really anything to say, you can say it here. I can spare you three minutes," she added, conclusively.

"Then let's walk around outside the railings. It's better than standing here; it won't look so odd if any one comes along who knows you," he said, and it seemed strange to her that he should

LONDON

have so much consideration for her. She was pleased. Her soul was of the order that delights to find others better than her mind had led her to expect. There are people, as you know, to whom it is always somewhat of a disappointment to find that any one is not so black as their fancy painted him. She turned and they walked slowly along the pavement that encircles the railings of the square garden.

"Well?" she said, "you said you had something to say to me."

"Yes, lots," he told her. "I was just trying to think which to say first. You know you've upset me a good deal. Oh, I forgive you, but it ought to be mutual. Yes, I'll put that first—I want us to forgive each other—forgive and forget and not bear grudge."

"Very well," she said, coldly. "I forgive you, but—"

He interrupted her before she could make the request that was on her lips. "That 'll do," he said. "Now, if you don't mind, I'm going to tell you how it was that I acted like a fool. I admit I acted like a fool," he added, handsomely. "I don't suppose I shall ever see you again and I don't want you to go on thinking me a perfect beast. I'd rather you didn't, though I know I was one that day, and I don't know why, but I would, even if I'm never to set eyes on you again. Well, you see, it's like this: I dare say it 'll sound silly to you, but even when I was at school I always wanted to do something noble—romantic, you know—rescuing ladies in distress, like Scott's novels, and things like that. I know it's too rotten for words, nowadays, what with machinery and telegraphs and radium and things, but that's what I used to think. And when I came up with you on the Seaford Road with no hat on and your poor little satin shoes all dusty and splitting, I thought, by Jove! my boy, here's your chance! And I did behave all right that day, didn't I?"

His voice was wistful, and she said, eagerly: "You were very, very kind. No one could have been nicer and more—more—"

"Respectful, eh? Well, I meant to be. I felt respectful; I do still. And you won't mind me saying I felt like a knight and you were the lady. I don't mean that you aren't a lady now, but you see what I mean, and you can't blame me if I thought it would all end in me and you being—well —you and me living happy ever after, the same as they do in books."

Enchanted by the revelation, she said, "Indeed, I don't blame you," more earnestly than she meant to do.

"Don't be too kind to me," he said, grimly. "I

know it doesn't mean anything, but it puts a man out. Well, then *he* came along, and you said he was your brother, and anybody could see with half an eye that he wasn't your brother; and I felt I'd been made a fool of, a complete, particular, first-class fool, and that put my back up. And I saw that things don't happen like they do in books. And I hadn't, somehow, thought you'd say anything that wasn't true."

She felt her face burn, and realized for the first time that in their brief and stormy acquaintance he had not been the only one to blame, and that, anyhow, it was she who had taken the first false step.

"I oughtn't to have told you a lie," she said, and added ingenuously, "especially after you'd been so kind; but I didn't know what to do—it seemed so difficult to explain." She could not tell him how difficult, nor why.

"Oh, that's all right," he said. "I should have said the same myself. It wasn't exactly a lie. It's a thing most people wouldn't make any bones about, only I thought you were different, that's all. And that was one of the things that made me feel it was fair to hunt you down, if I could—tit for tat, so to speak—and, besides, it was fun trying to see what I *could* find out. Then there's another thing I must tell you, I used to think it would be fun to be other things out of books—highwaymen and detectives and things—and I got a lead when I saw you at Cookham. After that I tracked you down like any old Sherlock Holmes, and I'm afraid at Kenilworth I behaved more like a highwayman than a respectable solicitor—for that's what I am."

"That's forgiven and forgotten," she told him.

"Well, I tracked you to Warwick, and when I saw your name in the visitors' book—Mr. and Mrs. Basingstoke—"

"But it wasn't—"

"It was, I assure you. Well, when I saw that I didn't know what to think, but I saw, however it was, it was all up with me; but I didn't want to see it, so I followed you to Kenilworth, and got a chance I didn't expect to behave like a cad and an ass, and behaved like them. But I don't think you know how pretty you are—and I didn't believe you were married, and all the things I'd thought while I was driving you to Tunbridge came up into my head and turned themselves inside out, somehow, and I felt what a fool I'd been, and I lost my head. And then you told me you wouldn't tell him, for fear he should hurt me; and that's really what I came here to say. That's what I can't stick. I can take care of myself. I want you to tell him anything you like—see?

Here's my card—and he can write to me, and I'll meet him anywhere he likes and let's see who's the best man. To set out to be a knight and all that, and end up with hiding behind a woman—and you to be the woman—no, I really can't stick it. So will you tell him?"

"I'll tell him everything," she said, "and he won't want to see who's the best man, and I don't want him to want it. And I don't want you to, either. You were a very kind knight-errant—but you weren't such a very good detective, or you'd have found out—"

"What?"

"I'll tell you, if you'll promise to give up wanting to find out who's the best man. Will you?"

"I'll do anything you like as long as you don't think I'm afraid of him, and don't let him think it, either. I don't think much of him, and I don't know whether you'll believe it, but it was that as much as anything set me to the detective business. I wanted to—to—I thought you wanted looking after. And then I acted like a brute—but I won't go on about that. Now tell me what it was I didn't find out?"

She pulled a little pale-silk bag from her pocket and took out a stiff folded paper and gave it to him. By the light of the next gas-lamp he un-

THE INCREDIBLE HONEYMOON

folded it; it was a long slip, partly printed, partly written. It was, in fact, the "marriage certificate" which had been obtained in order to quiet her family and to make possible the romance and adventure of the incredible honeymoon.

He glanced at it, folded it, and gave it back. "Thank you," he said. "I don't want to try who's the best man. He is. He's got you."

She could find nothing to say that should be at once true and kind.

"So that's all over," he said, straightening his shoulders. "There's only one thing more. You remember I went out to see about the car at Tunbridge, and I was rather a long time gone? Well, I rushed into a shop and bought this. I meant to throw it over Westminster Bridge as soon as I left you—but now, will you take it for a wedding-present? I'd like you to."

He fumbled at a spring, opened a case, and showed a half-hoop of sapphires.

"But I can't! It's too—"

"I'm *awfully* rich," he said, bitterly. "I've come into my father's business at Canterbury. I don't know what to do with my money, and the thing didn't cost much, really, but it was the best I could get. You believe that, don't you? And I thought it might be the beginning of living happy ever after, and I should like you to have it, just to show you really have forgiven me. You will, won't you?"

"I can't take the ring," she said, "but I wish I could, and I thank you very much for wishing me to have it—and for all your kindness and your kind thoughts of me."

"But you won't take the ring. He said you wouldn't."

"Who did?"

"My confessor. You see, I'm a Catholic, and I had to tell him about Kenilworth, and so I told him the whole thing. If it hadn't been for him I shouldn't have tried to tell you about it all and get you to forgive me. I'm glad I did, though."

Then she understood, and ceased to wonder how this man had got his poor, complicated, involved little history straightened out to such a convincing simplicity.

"I wish you'd have had the ring," he said again, discontentedly. "I never know what to do with my money."

"If I had a lot of money I'd go about the world trying to be a real knight-errant—just looking out for people who want things and don't ask for them—poor, proud, self-respecting people, poor schoolmasters and young men in shops who don't have good times. There was a man in a book who thought he was ill, and his doctor told him to help one person a day with his money. He got cured in no time; and you're not ill."

"I shouldn't know how to begin," he said. "You could have shown me, but you won't. Look here, don't go yet; stay a little and tell me how to begin."

Walking around and around the railings of the garden, she developed her thesis. They had been walking together for an hour and a half before they parted on her door-step, and at parting she did give him her hand.

In the hall she stood a minute or two, thinking. Then she slipped quietly out again and took an omnibus to Museum Street, and from there walked to Montague Street. She felt that the only important thing was to see Edward, to clear away the one cloud of concealment that lay between them—no, not the only one. The other was a very little thing; he, at least, had never known that it was there.

But when she reached number 37 it showed no light at any of its windows; only the basement window and the fanlight above the door gave out a dusky radiance. It seemed impossible to ring the bell and be faced with the assurance that he was not at home. So she walked slowly away.

And behind drawn curtains in the flower-scented, flower-bright room Charles stirred restlessly, and

LONDON

Edward, also restless, was saying, "I could almost believe that she would come to-night, now. All the rest of the time I have known in my heart that she would not come, but now, for the first time, it seems possible."

But the hours wore on and still he and the flowers and Charles were alone together.

XIX

HURSTMONCEAUX

THE sky was gray; gray mists veiled the sea and wisps of sea-fog lay in the hollows of the downs. The young morning had not yet decided whether it meant to be, when it was a grown-up day, a very wet day, when your umbrella is useless and you give it up and make up your mind to be wet through and change as soon as you get home; or a very fine day, one of those radiant, blazing days that are golden to the very end, days when you almost forget it ever has rained, and find it hard to believe that it will ever rain again. It was one of those mornings whose development is as darkly hid as the future of any babe smiling at you from its cradle and defying you to foresee whether it will grow up to be a great criminal or a great saint. If you love the baby, and trim its cradle with hopes and dreams, you will find it hard to believe that the darling can grow up just nobody in particular, like the rest of us.

To Edward, lying at his long length on the

short turf and looking out to the opalescent mist that hid the sea, it was not possible to believe that this day of all days could be anything but very good or very bad. The elements must be for him or against him, must help or hinder. That they could be indifferent was unthinkable.

For this was the day of days, come, at last, after weeks of a waiting that had not been patient, the day when he should, indeed, and not in dreams, see her again.

This was the thought, insistent, even in his sleep, that had at last broken up that sleep, as a trickle of water breaks up the embankment of a reservoir, letting out the deep floods inclosed by that barrier, the deep flood of pent-up longing which sleep could no longer restrain from consciousness.

So he had got up and come out to look over the sea and think of her.

Her letters made a bulge in his coat pocket; he pulled them out—a fat little bundle secured by an elastic band—and he read:

It is strange that you should have been expecting to see me just then, because just then I really had come as far as the door of your house—only everything was dark except for a murky star of gas that had been turned down in the hall. So I told myself that you weren't there, and I didn't want to be told so by any one else, and I went home. I like your letter; I like it very, very much, but it makes me see how stupid and selfish I have been to let you stay in London in the summer-time, waiting all the time for some one who never comes. And I want you to go away, right into the country, and I'll write to you as soon as Aunt Alice goes abroad. She is very, very much better. It won't be long now. A week, perhaps? Two weeks? Go away where it is green and glorious, and I shall think of you all the time and wish myself where you are.

At first when I read your letter I thought that I must see you just once before you go away. But now I see that I won't see you. If I were to see you it would not really make anything any easier. And nothing is very easy, as it is. You understand, don't you?

He hoped he did understand. If he understood, her letter meant the beginning of the end of the incredible honeymoon. For he dared to read the letter as he desired to read it, and where she had written, "If I were to see you it would not really make anything easier, and nothing is very easy," he had read, "If I were to see you I should find it too hard to part from you again," and next moment cursed himself for a presumptuous fool. What was he that the gods should now and thus renew to him an assurance that had once been his for a few magic hours, in the wild night-rush of a London-bound train, when the air was scented with the roses of dreams and the lady of all dreams slept upon his shoulder? For in those long and lonely days, in his London lodging, that assurance had dwindled, shriveled, faded to a maddening incertitude; the whole splendid pageant of his days had faded and shrunk to the pale substance of a vision.

Presumptuous or not, foolish or wise, the meaning which her letter might have revived his spirit, as the sweet air of dawn revives a man who comes out of a darkened prison to meet the waxing light and the first twitter of the newly awakened birds.

He had written:

I will go away—I will go away to the sea and wait there for you. You are right, as always. If I am not to see you it is less intolerable not to be near you. I hardly dare to read in your letter what I wish you could have meant me to read. But I warn you that when once I have you again I shall never let you go.

She had not answered that, though she had written every day, little, friendly, intimate notes, telling him of every day's little happenings and what were to be the happenings of the morrow. She told him, at last, that the aunt was really going, and when. She wrote:

The aunts are going to Scotland and I shall be left to see Aunt Alice off, and then, when she is gone, I will write and make an assignation with my friend and comrade, and we will go back to the good, green country. It won't be all different, will it? People meet again after years and don't recognize each other. I suppose they have been changing, changing a little bit every day. Do you think we shall have changed—contrariwise? You one way and I the other, I mean, so that when we do meet we sha'n't be the same?

The last letter of all was the shortest. "Monday," it said at the top of its page, and then:

Auntie leaves Folkestone to-morrow by the morning boat. I will let you know where to find me. Would Thursday suit you, in the afternoon?

He had felt no doubt as to that. Thursday would not suit him—but Tuesday would—and not the afternoon, but the morning. Had she really thought that he would wait two days?

And now, lying on the turf, he read her letters through and laid his face down on the last and dreamed a little, with closed eyes; and when he lifted his head again the mist had grown thin as a bridal veil and the sun was plain to be seen, showing a golden face above the sea, where a million points of light gleamed like tinsel through a curtain of gossamer. The air was warmer, the scent of the wild thyme sweeter and stronger, and overhead, in the gray that was growing every moment clearer and bluer, the skylarks were singing again.

"I knew," said Edward, as he went down toward the town where the smoke of the newly lighted fires rose straight from the chimneys—"I knew it couldn't have the heart not to be fine, on this day of all days."

He went back to his hotel and inspected once more certain of the purchases he had made since her decree had banished him from London. Resisting a momentary impulse toward asceticism in the matter of breakfast, as an outward and visible testimony to the unimportance of material things at such a time as this, he found himself at the other end of the pendulum's swing, ordering just such a meal as he would have ordered had she been with him, and ate his grape-fruit and omelette and delicately browned fish with thoughtful appreciation, making of them a banquet in her honor. He toasted her in the coffee, and, as he ate, romance insisted that it was not himself, but her man, whom he was treating to that perfectly served breakfast; and common sense added, "Yes, and no man's at his best if he's hungry." Before he reached the marmalade he had come to regard that impulse to tea and toast as a man might regard a vanished temptation to alcoholic excess.

"A hungry man's only half a man—the bad-tempered half," he said, lighting his first cigarette, and strolling out into the sunny inn-yard, where a hostler with a straw in his mouth was busy with a bucket of water and a horse's legs;

a pleasanter man, Edward thought, than the other man there, busy with oil and petrol and cotton-waste and a very new motor-car.

"I wish motors had never been invented," he told himself.

All the same, when the hour-glass of time had let through the last grain of the space of their separation, and a pale girl withdrew her eyes from the speck of a boat growing smaller and smaller on a sea that sparkled so brilliantly that you could hardly look at it, and almost listlessly turned to walk back alone to her hotel, she was confronted with a very pale young man standing beside a very new motor-car.

"You!" she said, and, as once before, the blood rushed to her face, and his to his, answering.

This was the moment for which he had lived for weeks—and they shook hands like strangers! She was grave and cold. What would her first words be?

"But I said Thursday," she said.

He looked like a criminal detected in a larceny.

"*I* said Tuesday," he told her. "Do you mind?"

In his anticipations of this moment he had always counted on a mutual wave of gladness in their reunion, in which all doubts should be resolved and all explanations be easy. Now, he himself felt awkward as a school-boy. And he noted in her a quite inexplicable restraint and embarrassment, although she was certainly saying that she did not mind, and that it did not matter at all.

"Where were you going?" he asked, mechanically, just for something to say as they stood there by the motor, jostled by all the people who had been seeing other people off.

"To my hotel, to pack and to write to you, as I said I would."

"Shall I go away and wait for the letter?" he asked, feeling that tea and toast would have done well enough.

"No. Don't be silly!" she said.

Now that the flush had died from her face he saw that it was paler and thinner. She saw in him a curious hardness. It was one of those moments when the light of life has gone out and there is nothing to be said that is not futile and nothing to be done that is of any use.

"It's a new car!" she said. "Yours?"

"Yes," he answered.

She wore a silky, soft-brown, holland-colored dress and a white hat with some black velvet about it and a dark rose. A wine-colored scarf fluttered about her, and in spite of her paleness and thinness she was more beautiful than ever and far more dear.

"Do you like the car?" he added, stupidly.

"Very much," she said, without so much as glancing at it. She looked up. "Well, what are we going to do?" she asked, almost crossly.

"Whatever you like."

"Oh dear!" her voice was plaintive. "You must have had *some* idea or you wouldn't have come to-day instead of Thursday. Hadn't you any idea, any scheme, any plan?"

"Yes," he said, "but it does not matter; I'll do anything you say."

"Oh, well," she said, "if you won't tell me your plans—" and she sketched the gesture of one who turns away and goes on her way alone.

"But I will," he said, quickly. Yet still he spoke like a very stupid child saying a lesson which it does not quite know. "I will tell you— I thought if you liked the car we might just get in and drive off—"

"Where?"

"Oh, just anywhere," he said, and hastened to add, "but I see now how silly it was. Of course I ought to have written and explained. Surprises are always silly, aren't they?"

And he felt as one who sits forlorn and feels the cold winds blow through the ruined arches of a castle in Spain. He had not read her letter as she had meant him to read it. Everything was different. Perhaps, after all, she did not—never had—he had deceived himself, like the fatuous fool he was.

"I ought to have thought," he blundered. "Of course you would not care to go motoring in that beautiful gown—and that hat—that makes you look like the Gardener's Daughter—'a sight to make an old man young'"—he added, recovering a very little—"and no coat! But I did buy a coat."

He leaned over and pulled out of the car a mass of soft brown fur lined with ermine. "Though, of course, it would have been better to ask you to choose one—I expect it's all wrong," and he heaved up the furry folds half-heartedly, without looking at her. "I just thought you might not have thought of getting one . . ." and his voice trailed away into silence, a silence that hers did not break.

Slowly she put out her hand and touched the fur, still without speaking. Then he did look at her, and suddenly the light of life sprang up again and the world was illumined from end to end. For her face that had been pale was pink as the wild rose is pink, and her mouth that had been sad was smiling; in her eyes was all, or almost all, that he had hoped to see there when, at last, after this long parting they should meet; and her hand was stroking the fur as if she loved it.

THE INCREDIBLE HONEYMOON

"It's the most beautiful coat in the world," she said, and her voice, like her face, was transfigured. She turned her shoulders to him that he might lay the coat on them, slipped her arms into the sleeves, and wheeled to confront him, her face alight with a mingled tenderness and gaiety that turned him, for a moment, faint and giddy.

"You really like it, Princess?" he faltered.

"I love it," she made answer; "and now, my lord, will you take me in your nice new motor-car to my unworthy hotel, that I may pay my miserable bill and secure my despicable luggage? Even a princess, you know, can't go to the world's end without a pair of slippers, a comb, and a clean pocket-handkerchief."

With that she was in the car, and he followed, gasping, in the sudden wave of enchantment that had changed the world. What had happened? Why had she suddenly changed? How had the cloud vanished? Whence had the cloud arisen?

His heart, or his vanity, or both, had been too bruised by the sudden blow to recover all in a minute. His brain, too, was stunned by the lack of any reason in what had happened. Why had she not been glad to see him? Why had she so suddenly turned from a cold stranger to her very self? What had worked the bad magic? Not, surely, the sight of a friend two days before she expected that sight? What had worked the good magic? It was not thinkable that any magic at all could be worked by a fur coat or even by the foresight that had provided it. His mind busied itself with such questions and felt no pain in them because it knew that his heart held in reserve, to be contemplated presently, the glorious fact that the good magic had, somehow, been wrought. But he would not call his heart into court yet. So that it was in silence that he drove through the steep streets. His own slight luggage was already at the back of the car, and when hers was added to it and they had left the town behind he still said nothing but the few words needed to such little matters as the disposing of the luggage and the satisfying of the hotel porter.

And when all the tall, stuccoed houses were left behind and they were rushing smoothly through the fresh morning, with the green sea on one side and the green marshland on the other, still he did not speak and kept his eyes on the white ribbon of road unrolling itself before him. It was just as they passed the third Martello tower that her hand crept under his arm. He took his from the steering-wheel for a moment to lay it on hers, and after that his heart had its way, and the silence, though still unbroken, was no longer the cloak for anxious questionings, but the splendid robe of a tender, tremulous joy.

They sped on; through Dymchurch, where the great sea-wall is, and where the houses are built lower than the sea, so that the high tide laps against the sea-wall level with the bedroom windows of the little houses that nestle behind its strong shelter.

It was she who spoke then. "Isn't it a dear little place?" she said. "Wouldn't you like to live in a Martello tower? They have one beautiful big room with a Norman-looking pillar in the middle, and a down-stairs part for kitchens, and an up-stairs, where the big gun is, that you could roof in for bedrooms. I should like a Martello! Don't you want to buy one? You know they built them to keep out Napoleon—and the canal as well—but no one uses them now. They just keep fishing-nets in them and wheelbarrows and eel-spears."

"Let's buy the haunted one," he said, and hoped that his voice was steady, for it was not of haunted towers that he desired to speak. "A soldier's ghost walks there; the village people say 'it's one of them there Roman soldiers that lived here when them towers was built in old ancient Roman times.'"

She laughed. "You know Dymchurch, then?

Isn't it nice when people know the same places? Almost as nice as it is when they've read the same books."

But the silence was not broken, only lifted. Her hand crept a little farther into the crook of his arm.

It was as they passed the spick-and-span white-painted windmill at New Romney that he said: "Don't you think it would be nicer to buy a windmill? There are four stories to that, and you can shift the top one around so that your window's always away from the wind."

"Yes," she said, "we really ought to buy a windmill."

The "we" lay warm at his heart until they came near Rye that stands upon its hill, looking over the marshes to the sea that deserted it so many years ago.

"There's a clock in Rye church that Sir Walter Raleigh presented to the town," he said, instructively.

"And Henry James lived there," said she.

"Shall we have lunch at the Mermaid Tavern? Or would you rather have a picnic? I've got a basket."

"How clever of you! Of course we'll have the picnic. And it's quite early. How beautifully the car is going!"

THE INCREDIBLE HONEYMOON

"Yes, isn't she?"

"Has she a name yet?"

"No. You must christen her."

"I should call her Time, because she flies so fast."

"You'd have to particularize. All time doesn't fly."

"No," she said, "ah, no! And she ought to have a splendid sort of name, she is so magnificently triumphant over space and time. Raleigh would have called her the 'Gloriana.'"

"So will we," said he. And they left Rye behind, and again the silence folded them round, and still her hand lay close in the crook of his arm.

At Winchelsea she suddenly asked, "Where's Charles?"

"Charles," he said, gravely, "is visiting my old nurse. He is well and happy—a loved and honored guest."

"The dear!" she said, absently. They were nearing Hastings before he spoke again, almost in a whisper, and this time what he said was what he meant to say.

"Are you happy?" he asked.

And she said, "Yes!"

It was at Hurstmonceaux that they opened the picnic basket—Hurstmonceaux, the great ruined Tudor castle, all beautiful in red brick and white stone. Less than a hundred years ago it was perfect to the last brick of it. But its tall old twisted red chimneys smoked. So a Hastings architect was called in. "I cannot cure your smoky chimneys, sir," said he, "but with the lead and some of the bricks of your castle I can build you a really comfortable and convenient modern house in the corner of your park, and I pledge you my word as an architect that the chimneys of the new house sha'n't smoke." So he did, and they didn't. And Hurstmonceaux was turned from a beautiful house to a beautiful ruin, and no one can live there; but parties of sightseers and tourists can be admitted on Mondays and Thursdays for a fee of sixpence a head, children half-price. All of which she read to him from the *Guide to Sussex*, as they sat in the grass-grown courtyard, where moss and wild flowers have covered the mounds of fallen brick.

"But this isn't Monday or Thursday," she said. "How did you get in?"

"You saw—with the big key, the yard of cold iron. I got special leave from the owner—for this."

"How very clever of you! How much better than anything *I* could have arranged."

"Approbation from Sir Hubert Stanley," he said, drawing the cork of the Rüdesheimer. "I do hope you *really* like lobster salad."

"And chicken and raspberries and cream, and everything. I like it all—and our dining-room—it's the most beautiful dining-room I ever had. I only thought of a wood, or a field, or perhaps a river, for Thursday."

"You did mean to have a picnic for Thursday?"

"Yes, but this is much better. It's a better place than I could have found, and besides—"

"Besides—?"

"It isn't Thursday."

When luncheon, a merry meal and a leisurely, was over, they leaned against a fallen pillar and rested their eyes on the beauty of green floor, red walls, and the blue sky roofing all. And above the skylarks sang.

"There's nothing between us now," he said, contentedly—"no cloud, no misunderstanding."

"No," she answered, "and I don't want there ever to be anything between us. So I'm going to tell you about Chester—the thing that worried me and I couldn't tell. Do you remember?"

"I think I do," he said, grimly.

"Only you must promise you won't be angry."

"With you?" he asked, incredulously.

"No . . . with him . . . and you must try to believe that it is true. No, of course not; I don't mean you're not likely to believe what *I* say, but what he said."

"Please," he pleaded, "I'm a patient man, but . . ."

So she told him the whole story of Mr. Schultz, and, at the end, waited for him to give voice to the anger that, from the very touch of his hand on hers, she knew he felt. But what he said was:

"It was entirely my fault. I ought never to have left you alone for an instant."

"You thought I was to be trusted," she said, a little bitterly, "and I couldn't even stay where you left me. But you do believe what he said?"

"I'll try to," he answered. "After all, he needn't have said anything—and if *you* believe it— Look here, let's never think of him or speak of him again, will you? We agreed, didn't we, that Mr. Schultz was only a bad dream, and that he never really happened. And there's nothing now between us at all . . . no concealments?"

"There's one," she said, in a very small voice, "but it's so silly I don't think I *can* tell you."

"Try," said he. "I could tell of the silliest things. And after that there's one more thing I wish you'd tell me, if you can. You *are* happy, aren't you? You are glad that we're together again?"

"Yes," she said. "Oh yes!"

"And this morning you weren't?"

"Oh, but I was, I was! It was only— That's

THE INCREDIBLE HONEYMOON

the silly thing I want to tell you. But you'll laugh."

"It wasn't a laughing matter to me."

"I know I was hateful."

"It was—bewildering. I couldn't understand why everything was all wrong and then, suddenly, everything was all right."

"I know—I was detestable. I can't think how I could. But, you see, I was disappointed. I meant to arrange for you to meet me at some very pretty place and I was going to have a very pretty luncheon. I'd thought it all out . . . and it was exactly the same as yours, almost, only I shouldn't have known the name of the quite-perfect wine and, then . . . there you were, you know, and I hadn't been able to make things nice for you."

"Was that really all, my Princess?"

"Yes, that was all."

"But still I don't understand why everything was suddenly all right."

"It was what you said. That made everything all right."

"What I said?"

"You see, I meant it all to be as pretty as I could make it, and I'd got a new dress, very, very pretty, and a new hat . . . and then you came upon me, suddenly, in this old rag and last year's hat and scarf I only wore because aunty gave them to me. And I felt caught, and defrauded, and . . . and dowdy."

"Oh, Princess!"

"And then you said . . . you said you liked my dress . . . so, then, it did not matter."

It was then that he lifted her hand to hold it against his face as once before he had held it, and silence wrapped them around once more—a lovely silence, adorned with the rustle of leaves and grass and the skylark's passionate song.

XX

THE END

THE memory of luncheon died away and the picnic-basket, again appealed to, yielded tea. They had explored the towers, and talked of Kenilworth, the underground passages, and talked of the round tower of Wales. And half their talk was, "Do you remember?" and, "Have you forgotten?" The early days of the incredible honeymoon had been days of exploration, each seeking to discover the secrets of that unknown land, each other's mind and soul; this day of reunion was one gladly given over to the contemplation of the memories they had together amassed. It was a day dedicated to the counting of those treasures of memory which they now held in common, treasures among which this golden day itself would, all too soon, have to be laid aside to be, for each of them, forever, the chief jewel of that priceless treasury.

It was when they were repacking the picnic-

THE END

basket that they first noticed how the color had gone out of the grass, that was their carpet, and how the blue had faded from the sky, that was their roof. The day had changed its mind, after all. Having been lovely in its youth and glorious in its prime, it had, in its declining hours, fallen a prey to the grayest melancholy and was now very sorry for itself indeed.

"Oh dear!" said she, "I do believe it's going to rain."

Even as she spoke the first big tears of the dejected day fell on the lid of the teapot.

"We must hurry," he said, briskly. "I can't have my princess getting wet through and catching cold in her royal head. Run for it, Princess! Run to the big gateway!"

She ran; he followed with the basket, went out to cover the seats of his car with mackintosh rugs and put up the hood, and came back, dampish, to discuss the situation. They told each other that it was only a shower, that it couldn't possibly, as they put it, have "set in." But it had; the landscape framed in the arch of the gateway lost color moment by moment, even the yellow of the gorse was blotted and obscured; the rain, which at first had fallen in a fitful, amateurish sort of way, settled down to business and fell in gray, diagonal lines, straight and sharp as ramrods.

THE INCREDIBLE HONEYMOON

"And it's getting late," he said, "and your Highness will be hungry."

"We've only just had tea," she reminded him.

"Ah, but we've got some way to go," he told her.

"Where *are* we going?"

"I had thought," he said, "of going to a place beyond Eastbourne; . . . my old nurse lives there. She's rather fond of me; . . . she'll have gotten supper for us. I thought you'd like it. It's a farm-house, rather a jolly one, and then I thought, if you liked, we could drive back to the Eastbourne hotel by moonlight."

"That would have been nice."

"But there won't be any moonlight. Perhaps we'd better go straight to the hotel."

"But your nurse will expect you."

"I can telegraph."

"But she'll be so disappointed."

"Why didn't I get a car that would shut up and be weather-tight? The rain will drift under that hood like the deluge."

She laughed. "A little rain won't hurt us."

"Your beautiful hat!"

"I'll tie my ugly scarf around my head and put my beautiful hat under the rug. Come, don't let us disappoint your old nurse. No! It's not going to leave off; it's only taking breath to go on harder than ever."

THE END

It was said afterward that never, in the memory of the oldest inhabitant, had there been such a storm of rain in those parts—rain without thunder, rain in full summer, rain without reason and without restraint. The rain drifted in, as he had said it would, and abruptly a wild wind arose and tore at the hood of the car, flapped her scarf in her eyes, and whipped their faces with sharp, stinging rain. He stopped at the village inn and brought her out ginger-brandy in a little glass shaped like a thistle-flower, "to keep the cold out." Also he went into the post-office and bought peppermint bull's-eyes, "to keep us warm," he said. "How admirably fortunate that we both like peppermint!" And the journey began in earnest, up hills that were torrents, through hollows that were ponds, where the water splashed like a yellow frill from their wheels as they rushed through it. One village street was like a river, and the men were busy with spades, digging through the hedge-banks channels by which the water might escape into the flooded fields.

And so, along through Pevensey, where the great Norman castle still stands gray and threatening, through Eastbourne, like an ant-heap where the ants all use umbrellas, and, at long last, out on to the downs. Her hands were ice-cold with the rain and the effort of holding mackintosh rugs about herself and him. Her hair was blown across her eyes, the lash of rain was on her lips. Breathless, laughing for the joy of the wild rush through wind and water, they gained the top of Friston Hill, where the tall windmill is, and the pond and the sign-post and the small, gray, quiet church. And here, as suddenly as it had begun, the rain ceased; the clouds drifted away.

"As though some great tidy angel had swept them up with his wings," said she.

The sea showed again, gray with chalk stolen from the cliffs, and white with the crests of waves left angry by the wind. Under the frowning purple clouds in the west glowed a long line of sullen crimson, and they went on along the down road in the peace of a clear, translucent twilight. Below them, in a hollow, shone lights from a little house.

"Wasn't it somewhere here," she asked him, "that you left me and I didn't stay?"

"Yes," he said, "somewhere here."

And then they had reached the house—not so little, either, when you came close to it—and there were steady lights shining through the lower windows, and, in the upper rooms, the fitful, soft glimmer of firelight. The car stopped at the wooden gate from which a brick path led to the front door, hospitably open, showing gleams of

THE END

brass and old mahogany in a wide hall paved with black-and-white checkered marble.

He peeled the streaming waterproof from her shoulders and gave her his hand for the descent. Side by side they passed down the wet path between dripping flower-beds, but at the threshold he stepped before her, entered the house, and turned to receive her.

"Welcome!" he said, caught her by the elbows, and lifted her lightly over the threshold.

"Why did you do that?" she asked, breathless and smiling through the drift of wet, disordered tresses.

"It's an old custom for welcoming a princess," he said.

The old nurse came from the kitchen, rustling in stiff print and white apron.

"Oh, Master Edward, sir," she said, beaming, "I never thought you'd come in all this rain, not even when I got the telegraph. Nicely, ma'am, thanking you kindly and hoping you're the same," she said, in answer to the greeting and the hand that the girl offered. "And your good lady, Master Edward, she must be wet through, but I've got a lovely fire in her room, if you'll come along with me, ma'am, and I'll bring up some hot water in two ticks."

So now, after the wind and the rain and the car,

the girl finds herself in a long, low, chintz-curtained room where a wood fire burns on an open hearth and a devoted nurse of his is pulling off wet shoes and offering cups of tea and hot water.

"And are you quite sure there ain't nothing more I can do for you, ma'am, for I'm sure it's a pleasure?"

The girl, left alone at last, found herself wondering. He must have felt very sure of her, surely, to have brought her thus to his nurse, as if . . . as if their marriage had been a real marriage, like other people's.

"Well, and why shouldn't he be sure of me?" she asked herself. "I'm sure of him, thank God!"

The appointments about her were so charming, all so perfectly in keeping with one another and with the room that held them, that she found herself making a comfortable, complete, and ceremonious toilette. She had with her, by a fortunate accident, as she told herself, a dress of soft, cream-colored India muslin, fine as gauze. But when she looked at herself in the glass she said, "Too white . . . it's like a wedding-dress," and sought for some color to mitigate the dress's bridal simplicity. There was no scarf that quite stifled criticism, but there was the Burmese coat, long and red, with gold-embroidered hems a foot deep. She slipped it over the white gown and was satisfied.

THE END

She thought of the morning when she had last worn the Burmese coat, and "He liked the red rose," she said, as she put it on. When she was dressed she sat down in the great arm-chair before the fire and rested, tasting the simple yet perfect luxury of it all. She did not know how long she sat there, and reverie had almost given place to dreaming when a tap at the door aroused her.

She opened it. Edward stood there.

"Shall we go down to supper?" he said, exactly as though they had been at a dance. And, indeed, they might have been at a dance, as far as their dress went, except that he wore a dinner-jacket in place of the tail-coat which dances demand.

He offered his arm, and she took it and they went together down the shallow, wide, polished, uncarpeted stairs on which the lamps from the corridor above threw the shadows of the slender, elegant balustrades.

"What a beautiful house!" she said. "And how nice of you to make yourself pretty for supper!"

"Well, we had to change into something, and I won't attack you with the obvious rejoinder. But you'll let me say, won't you, that you're like a princess in a fairy-tale? Did your fairy godmother give you a hundred dresses at your christening, each one more beautiful than the other?"

"She gave me something," the girl answered—"a secret amulet. It's invisible, but it brings me good fortune. It's brought me here," she added, "where everything is perfect. My room's lovely, and those stuffed sea-gulls over there . . . nothing else could have been absolutely right in that recess. How odd that I never knew before how much I loved stuffed sea-gulls," she added, meditatively.

He stopped in front of the sea-gulls. "I got a ring for you at Warwick," he said, "only I didn't dare to ask you to take it. Will you take it now? The other one was the symbol of something you didn't mean. Let this one stand for—whatever you will."

Without a word she held out her hand, so he set the diamond and crystal above the golden circlet.

"I am a fairy princess," she said then. "No one but a fairy princess ever had such a ring as this. Thank you, my Prince."

With the word, planted on the hour like a flag, they went on.

The dining-room was paneled with beech, gray and polished. In the middle a round table spread with silver and glass, white lawn and white roses, shone like a great wedding-cake.

"Do you mind," he said, as he set the chair for

THE END

her—"do you mind if we make it another picnic and wait on ourselves? My old nurse was anxious to get back to her babies—she's got five of them—so I ran her down in the car."

"She lives in the village, then? I thought she lived here."

"I thought the five children might be rather too much for you, especially when you're so tired."

"But I'm not," she said, "and oh, what a pretty supper!"

The curtains were drawn, wax candles shone from Sheffield-plated candlesticks on table and mantelpiece and gleamed reflected in china and silver and the glass of pictures and bookcases. A little mellow fire burned on the hearth.

"What a darling room!" she said, "and how all the things fit it, every single thing, exactly right. They couldn't go any other way, possibly."

"You told me they would," he said, "at Warwick. I remember you told me they would fit in if one only loved them and gave them the chance. I drink to you, Princess; and I know sparkling wine is extravagant; but to-day isn't every day, and it's only Moselle, which is not nearly so expensive as champagne, and much nicer."

Raising their glasses, they toasted each other.

"But I thought," she said, presently—"I thought—there were to be no concealments."

THE INCREDIBLE HONEYMOON

"No more there are."

"But this isn't . . . Isn't this . . . Surely that's the bookcase you bought at Warwick—and these chairs and those candlesticks."

"I own it, Princess; I would scorn to deceive you."

"Then this is *your* house?"

"It is; just that."

"Only that? Is there nothing else that it is? Wasn't it once my house, for a very little while? Wasn't it here that you left me, that night when I ran away and I met Mr. Schultz? . . . No, I forgot. . . . Of course I didn't meet any one. . . . I mean when you came after me and found me at Tunbridge Wells. Oh! Suppose you hadn't found me!"

"How am I to suppose the impossible? You couldn't be in the same world with me and I not find you. Yes, you are right, as always; this is the house. Did you ever try bananas with chicken? Do! They rhyme perfectly."

"Don't seek to put me off with bananas. Was the house yours when you brought me here?"

"Yes; I had just bought it. All concealment is really at an end now. And I am rather glad I did buy it, because this is certainly better than the coffee-room of an inn, isn't it?"

"How proud he is of his house! And well he

THE END

may be! And when did he arrange all this beautiful furniture?"

"When she banished him from London. It was something to do; and she does like it?"

"She does indeed. Have you furnished it all?"

"Not nearly all. I wanted your advice about the other parlor and the housekeeper's room and—oh, lots of things. Yes, you are quite right in the surmise which I see trembling on those lips. Mrs. Burbidge is going to be our housekeeper. She's staying at old nurse's, ready to come in whenever she's wanted. If any one else decides to keep house for me she can be sewing-maid, or still-room maid, or lady-in-waiting to the hen-roost."

"I see," she said, crumbling bread and looking at him across the glass and the silver and the white flowers. "So this was the house! When I was in the straw nest you made me I never thought the house could be like this. I imagined it damp and desolate, with strips of torn paper—ugly patterns —hanging from the wall, and dust and cobwebs and mice, perhaps even a rat. I was almost sure I heard a rat!"

"Poor, poor little princess."

"Yes, I will!" she said, suddenly, answering a voice that was certainly not his. "I don't care what you say, I *will* tell him. Edward, when I ran away it wasn't only because I didn't want to be a burden and all that—though that was true, too—the real true truth was that I was frightened. Yes, I was! I shivered in that straw nest and listened and listened and listened, and held my breath and listened again, and I was almost sure I heard something moving in the house; and it was so velvet-dark, and I had to get up every time I wanted to strike a match, because of not setting fire to the straw, and at last there were only four matches left. And I kept thinking—suppose something should come creeping, creeping, very slowly and softly, through the darkness, so that I shouldn't know it until it was close to me and touched me! I couldn't bear it—so I ran away. Now despise me and call me a coward."

But he only said, "My poor Princess, how could I ever have left you alone for a moment?" and came around the table expressly to cut just the right number of white grapes for her from the bunch in the silver basket. Being there, his hand touched her head, lightly, as one might touch the plumage of a bird.

"How soft your hair is!" he said, in a low voice, and went back to his place.

When the meal was over, "Let's clear away," she said, "it won't look so dismal for your nurse when she comes in the morning."

"Let me do it," said he. "Why should you?"

THE END

"Ah, but I want to," she said. "And I want to see the kitchen."

And the kitchen was worth seeing, with its rows of shining brasses, its tall clock, its high chintz-flounced mantelpiece. When all was in order, when the table shone bare in its bright, dark mahogany, he mended the fire, for the evening was still chill with the rain, and drew up the big chair for her to the hearth she had just swept. He stood a moment looking down at her.

"May I sit at your feet, Princess?" he asked.

She swept aside her muslin and her gold embroideries to make a place for him. The house was silent, so silent that the crackle of the wood on the hearth seemed loud, and louder still the slow ticking of the tall clock on the other side of the wall. Outside not a breath stirred, only now and then came the tinkle of a sheep-bell, the sound of a hoof on the cobblestones of the stable across the yard, or the rattle of the ring against the manger as some horse, turning, tossed his head.

He leaned back against her chair and threw his head back until he could look at her face. The tips of her fingers touched his forehead lightly and his head rested against her knee; and now he could not see her face any more. Only he felt those smooth finger-tips passing across his brow with the touch of a butterfly caress.

THE INCREDIBLE HONEYMOON

"Are you happy?" he said, once again and very softly.

And once again she answered, "Yes!"

Her hand ceased its movement and lay softly on his hair. His hand came up and found her other hand. For a long time neither spoke. Then suddenly she said, "What is it?" for she had felt the tiniest movement of the head her hand rested on, a movement that told her he had been about to speak and had then thought, "Not now, not yet."

So she said, "What is it?" because she had a secret, and she feared that he knew it.

Then he did speak. He said: "I have something to tell you; I hope you will forgive me. I must tell you now. Ah! let your hand lie there while I tell you. Princess, I have deceived you. If I did not think you would forgive me, I don't think I could tell you, even now."

"I could forgive you anything," she said, so low that he hardly knew he heard it.

"It is this," he said. "That marriage of ours—that mock marriage—ah, try to forgive me for deceiving you! It was a real marriage, my dear; I tricked you into a real marriage. It seemed to be the only way not to lose you. It was a real marriage. You are my wife."

The clock ticked on in the kitchen, the fire

THE END

crackled on the hearth, far on the down a sheep-bell tinkled and was still. He sat there, immobile, rigid, like a statue of a man, his heart beating a desperate tune of hope and fear. Could she forgive him? Dared he hope it? This moment, so long foreseen, held terrors he had not foretold for it. Was it possible that this deceit of his should come between them, even now? He almost held his breath in a passion of suspense, and the moments fell past slowly, slowly. He could bear it no longer. He sprang up, walked across the room, came back, leaned on the mantelpiece so that she could not see his face.

"Oh, Princess, oh, my dearest!" he said, brokenly, "don't say that you can't forgive me."

She, too, had risen and stood beside him. Now she laid her hand on his shoulder. "It's not that," she said. "I don't know how to tell you. I've nothing to forgive—unless you have, too."

He turned to meet her eyes, and they fell before his.

"Oh, Edward," she said, with a little laugh that was half tears, "don't look like that! My dear, I knew it all the time."

And there they were, clinging to each other like two children saved from a shipwreck.

"You knew?" he said at last.

"Of course I knew," she said.

THE INCREDIBLE HONEYMOON

They drew back to let their eyes meet in that look of incredulous gladness that lovers know when, at last, all barriers are down and true love meets true love without veils or reservations.

"Thank God for this day," he said, reverently.

And at that a thunderous clamor at the house-door broke in on their dream, a clatter and a clangor, a rattling of chains and a volley of resonant reverberatory barks.

"Why, it's Charles!" he cried. "How could he know I was here?"

How, indeed? For it was indeed Charles, incredibly muddy and wet, bounding round in the room the moment the doors were opened, knocking over a chair, clattering the fire-irons, and coming to heavy anchor, with all four feet muddy, on the edge of her white gown.

"I must go and chain him up in the stable," he said, when Charles had been fed with the remains of the supper. "You won't be afraid to be left alone in the house, Princess, dear?"

"I sha'n't be afraid now," she said, caressing Charles's bullet head. "You see, it's all different now. How could I be afraid in my own home?"

THE END